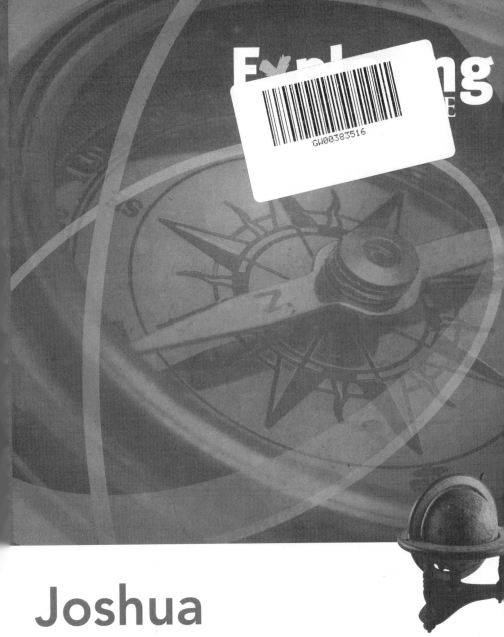

GW00383516

Joshua
A devotional commentary

Colin N Peckham

DayOne

© Day One Publications 2007
First printed 2007

ISBN 978–1–84625–093–4

Unless otherwise indicated, Scripture quotations are from the **New King James Version (NKJV)®**. Copyright © 1982 by Thomas Nelson, Inc. Used by permission. All rights reserved.

British Library Cataloguing in Publication Data available

Published by Day One Publications
Ryelands Road, Leominster, HR6 8NZ
☎ 01568 613 740 FAX 01568 611 473
email—sales@dayone.co.uk
web site—www.dayone.co.uk
North American—email—sales@dayonebookstore.com
North American—web site—www.dayonebookstore.com

Designed by Steve Devane and printed by Gutenberg Press, Malta

If you are looking for a fast moving, down-to-earth and challenging insight into Joshua, then this is it. Colin Peckham presents a grasp of the book that is easy to take in, particularly the long historical chapters, and manages at the same time to show how the book's message is just as vital for today as it has always been. Buy it, study it and act upon it.

—Rev. Dr A M Roger, Principal, The Faith Mission Bible College, Edinburgh

Thank God for this delightful, scriptural and deeply devotional commentary. It will make the book of Joshua and its spiritual wealth come alive for you. It is so readable that it seems like a series of inspiring messages by a godly Bible teacher. You forget that it is also a very worthwhile, thoroughly researched and detailed devotional commentary. God intends for us to read and be blessed and guided by the book of Joshua, and much more of the Old Testament, far more than is the case for many Christians. This book will encourage many to read the Old Testament more fully than has been their custom. May God use it widely.

Dr Peckham is a writer whose Christian passion will bless and inspire you. You will desire to underline many places as you read, for you will go back again and again. Read it through in its entirety.

—Dr Wesley Duewel, President Emeritus of The OMS International, and author

For some years I have been encouraging Dr Colin Peckham to add a Bible commentary to his other published works and I am delighted he has produced this excellent commentary on the book of Joshua. I have found it true to the text, devotional and challenging in spirit, and practical in application. Even though Joshua is an Old Testament book, its truth is relevant for the people of God today. May God make it a great blessing to all who read and study it.

—Rev. Tom Shaw, Former President of The Faith Mission, and Minister of Donaghey Congregational Church, N. Ireland

Appreciations

'There is a point in grace as much above the ordinary Christian as the ordinary Christian is above the worldling,' said the nineteenth-century Baptist preacher, Charles Haddon Spurgeon. His comments capture the heart cry of this series of studies in Joshua from the respected pen of Dr Colin Peckham. He wants us to see not merely Jericho but Jesus, not only the Land but supremely the Lord. I was humbled, challenged and refreshed by it. You will be too.

—Dr Steve Brady, Principal, Moorlands College, and Trustee, Keswick Convention

No book of the Old Testament teaches more clearly the principles of victory in the midst of battle, and rest in the midst of struggle than the book of Joshua. From this background, Colin Peckham applies these truths magnificently to create an appetite for victorious living and to show the means of experiencing this through full surrender to Christ as Lord, and complete dependence on him as our strength. Here is the gospel for defeated and struggling Christians, a gospel that does not only get us out of the old life of slavery to leave us wandering in a wilderness of confusion, but brings us into the new life of a land 'flowing with milk and honey'—the fullness of Christ.

—Dr Charles Price, The People's Church, Toronto, Canada

Dr Peckham has produced a great book which perfectly blends together doctrine, devotion and dedication. This is a book for our times for pastor and people alike—a book to be read and re-read.

Our day has forgotten the vision of victory set forth in this book. Without such a vision the people will perish and a defeated church will never conquer the world, the flesh, or the devil. Here is a challenge for us to blow upon the gospel trumpets and shout, for the Lord has given us our cities which, like wicked Jericho, are shut up and need their walls of opposition and indifference to crumble before God's victorious battle-cry.

The book of Joshua is a book for today, and the message of this volume is timely and blessed.

—Rev. Paul Bassett, Minister, Melbourne Hall Evangelical Free Church, Leicester, England

Dedication

I dedicate this book to the memory of my beloved parents, Ivan and Doris Peckham of New Hanover, Natal, South Africa, who, when God called me into his service, never stood in my way despite the cost involved, but helped in every way they could to enable me to fulfil my calling. Mum and Dad, you are still in my heart—Thank you!

And to the memory of dear 'Aunt Mackie', that godly soul who had such an impact upon my young life, and made it easy for me to follow Jesus.

Contents

Contents

Maps

The book of Joshua is a significant bridge between the early historical books of the Bible—the Pentateuch—and the records of Israel's development as a nation under the judges and then the kings. The people faced remarkable challenges—and were able to overcome in the strength and goodness of God, who daily upheld them.

There are many parallels between the history of the times of Joshua and the way we face spiritual obstacles and challenges as we live in the context of the teaching of both the Old and New Testaments. Did they face giants? So do we, albeit of a different kind! Were they challenged to do things by faith rather than by sight? So, too, must we! Did they struggle before they came to victory? So, too, it is in our experience.

In this devotional commentary, I draw many lines of application between the circumstances of the Israelites and our modern-day experiences of the Christian life. These studies will hopefully be beneficial and of great help. They are intended to be thrilling, inspiring and challenging as they are applied to heart and life. The object has been to draw God's people into a closer experience with him.

I humbly submit it to God's people everywhere, praying that many will find deliverance and joy, victory and stability, inspiration and blessing as they exercise faith in God.

Rev. Dr. Colin N. Peckham L.Th. Hons, B.A., B.Th. (Hons), M.Th, D.Th.
Edinburgh, 2007

1 **Entering the land (1:1–5:12)**
   a. **The preparation of the people (1:1–3:13)**
      i The inward preparation—the law (1:1–18)
         The Lord speaks to Joshua
         Joshua speaks to the people
         The people speak to Joshua
      ii The outward preparation—the spies (2:1–24)
         The mission of the spies
         The covenant of the spies
         The report of the spies
      iii The onward preparation—the ark (3:1–13)
   b. **The passage of the people (3:14–4:24)**
      i The crossing of Jordan
      ii The memorial in Jordan
      iii The encampment over Jordan
   c. **The purification of the people (5:1–12)**
      i The consternation of the enemy
      ii The circumcision of the sons
      iii The cessation of the manna
2 **Conquering the land (5:13–12:24)**
   a. **The revelation of victory (5:13–15)**
   b. **The realization of victory (6:1–11:23)**
      i The central campaign—Jericho, Ai
      ii The southern campaign—Gibeon, Beth Horon
      iii The northern campaign—Merom
   c. **The record of victory (12)**
      i East of Jordan
      ii West of Jordan
3 **Possessing the land (13:1–24:33)**
   a. **Distribution of the land among the tribes (13:1–21:45)**
      i Possession of the two and a half tribes (13)

ii Possession of Caleb (14)

iii Possession of the nine and a half tribes (15–19)

iv The cities of refuge (20)

v The cities of the Levites (21)

b. Dispute about an altar upon the border (22:1–34)

i The charges (vv. 1–20)

ii The clearance (vv. 21–29)

iii The conclusion (vv. 30–34)

c. Discourse and death of Joshua (23:1–24:33)

i The first address (23)

ii The second address (24:1–28)

iii The three graves (24:29–33)

Jordan

Redeemed by the blood of the Lamb, on the door,
From bondage at last they were free.
They walked to the water to hear the waves roar,
But God led them right through the sea.

Rebellious in heart they did not obey,
They knew not his promise of rest;
Their idols held sway in the wearisome way
Of the great, howling wilderness.

'Go up,' they were urged, 'and now take the land,
The land to which God leads you.'
'Walled cities before us and giants take their stand
Preventing us following through.'

They died in the desert! their bones bleached and white;
They died for they would not believe.
God promised the land which was now in their sight,
But his conquest they could not achieve.

Then Moses—the Law—was taken at last,
A new Man they had at their head;
And on in their journeys, with victories past,
To the river of death he them led.

The ark was a picture of Christ in each part,
It was borne to the waters' expanse—
'What ails you, O Jordan? And why do you flee?'

For the waters retreated at once.

It stood in the river! Victorious o'er death!
It stood till they all were gone through!
From the dry arid wastes to the long-promised place
By the death and the rising anew.

And so in identification with him
We die to the wilderness life
Of jealousies, pride, the uncleanness we hide,
Carnality, envy and strife.

The cross is the door to deliverance in him!
We die with him, yet in him live;
Abundance of life in this Canaan of love
Is the fullness of grace that he gives.

Rejoice then and trust him, and take from his hand
The blessings of Canaan above
When God leads in victory to conquer the land
Where we live and abide in his love.

Colin N. Peckham

The book of Joshua

The book of Joshua describes the invasion, conquest, division and possession of the land of Canaan by Israel as a unified national group organized into twelve tribes under the leadership of Joshua, the successor to Moses. It is a record of the happenings during the life of Joshua while he was the leader of the nation, a period of about twenty-five years. It opens with the death of Moses and the call of Joshua, and ends with the death of Joshua.

A bridge book

Joshua is a book of transition; a transition from the patriarchal age when the nation of Israel was called, delivered and trained, to the age of settled occupation of the land. It is not until Joshua that we have the fulfilment of the promise which God gave to Abraham in Genesis 12:7, that he would give them this land.

The books of Moses precede this writing. Genesis is the book of *beginnings*; Exodus is the book of *redemption*; Leviticus is the book of *fellowship and worship*; Numbers is the book of the *walk and wanderings* of the Israelites; and Deuteronomy is the book of *obedience*, for there the second law was given. The book of Joshua records the period of Israel's establishment as a nation of which Genesis was prophetic and the Pentateuch as a whole was preparatory. The books of Moses would be incomplete and imperfect without Joshua, and the history which followed it would be unexplained. The book of Joshua is the indispensable link. It bears the same relationship to the five books of Moses as the book of Acts bears to the four Gospels.

The date of the book

The actual date of the Exodus from Egypt has been a problem for scholars for centuries and has not been resolved. Two specific dates are singled out as being more significant than others: 1240 BC and 1441 BC. The latter date would point to 1400 BC for the invasion of Canaan; this is perhaps the most likely date.

The writer of the book

According to the Talmud (the body of Jewish law), 'Joshua wrote his own book', but there continues to be controversy over the authorship of the book. Scripture does not identify the author and there is no conclusive evidence that Joshua wrote it. Although the human authorship may be debatable, the divine inspiration is clear. Throughout the book God has a very active role. He is the One who took the initiative for the moves made by Israel. The divine element is magnified, so the spiritual emphasis of the book must be given its proper emphasis.

Internal factors indicate that the writer lived at the time of Joshua, for example, 'until we had crossed over' (Joshua 5:1)—the 'we' giving a sense of corporate solidarity and eyewitness clarity.

The phrase 'to this day' is often used, for example, 'Rahab ... dwells in Israel to this day' (6:25). This expression could, of course, have been used by a writer fifty years after Joshua and is therefore not conclusive.

However, Jewish tradition would probably be correct in attributing the authorship of the book to Joshua himself. We read: 'Then Joshua wrote these words in the Book of the Law of God' (24:26).

The book certainly could not have been written after David, for the Jebusites were still living in Jerusalem (15:63) and it was David who drove them out (2 Samuel 5:6–7).

Joshua obviously did not write all of the book, as his own death is recorded in the last chapter.

The theme of the book

The book is one of conflict and conquest, of military prowess, of joyful optimism, victory and action. The people were marching forward under Joshua's leadership to possess the land which had been promised to their fathers. We have stories of aggressive military campaigns and of amazing victories.

The characteristics of the book

The book's primary message is the *faithfulness of God*. It demonstrates that God kept the promises which he made to Abraham. The people were to possess the land which he had promised them.

It also speaks of the *holiness of God*. The iniquity of the Amorites was now full (Genesis 15:16) and the land was to be swept clean of all the sin of the nations which possessed it. God wants a clean and holy people.

It further shows *God's great salvation* to be one of victory, stability and rest. It symbolizes the life of the fullness of blessing to which the Captain of the Lord's host brings us. The book of Joshua foreshadows truths which have their fulfilment in the New Testament. Ephesians and Joshua go hand in hand as they both teach the attaining of that which God has promised; Joshua is a type, symbolizing the spiritual inheritance in Christ that is explained particularly in Ephesians.

It introduces a *new method of teaching*. Up to this time God had spoken to his people in dreams and visions, but now they have the Book of the Law of Moses. They are exhorted to obey God through the book.

The key verse of the book

So Joshua took the whole land, according to all that the LORD had said to Moses; and Joshua gave it as an inheritance to Israel according to their divisions by their tribes. Then the land rested from war (11:23).

Here we see:
- The conquest: 'So Joshua took the whole land.'
- The fulfilment of promise: 'according to all that the LORD had said to

Moses.'

- The allotment to the people: 'and Joshua gave it as an inheritance to Israel according to their divisions by their tribes.'
- The rest: 'Then the land rested from war.'

The problem of the book

The book of Joshua touches a raw nerve in most people, who recoil from its chronicle of the brutal conquest of an indigenous population, deliberate acts of genocide, and ethnic cleansing. Joshua is the product of his own age and culture, but the final answer to this problem is God's hatred for the sin of the people in the land.

Until the discovery of the Ugarit tablets in the early part of the twentieth century, we had no idea of the extent to which the religious system in the land of Canaan had corrupted itself. Now, because of these tablets, we can see the demonic, licentious worship system which had evolved. Baal worship was a combination of sexual activity, with male or female prostitutes in the Baal temple, and human sacrifice, particularly of their children. Also, the influence of the Egyptian pantheon could be felt across the whole region.

God was offended to the point of commanding the total extermination of the inhabitants of the land of Canaan. Should any remain, they would corrupt the true religion of Yahweh. 'You shall utterly destroy them ... lest they teach you to do according to all their abominations' (Deuteronomy 20:16–18). The time for their judgement had come.

Perhaps we have difficulty with this problem because we have so little knowledge of the holiness of God; for God sees sin in all its wickedness. God can do nothing else but destroy it and show that the people whom he is introducing to the land must be pure and holy.

The man Joshua

Moses' household

WHY JOSHUA?

Why did Joshua succeed Moses as leader of the people? Where were Moses' two sons, Gershom and Eliezer? Surely they had had the privileged position of living with the great man, drawing from his wisdom, observing his ways and being trained for leadership? Were they both dead? Had they turned away from their father's God and become rebellious and untrustworthy? Had Moses failed to give enough time to the development of his own sons, so that they disregarded his leadership and went their own way? Had the work of God been so burdensome that Moses had had no time for the swiftly passing opportunities of bringing up his own boys? Had he failed as a father? Were his household now paying the price of that failure?

Or was Moses' house divided? Were Miriam and Aaron right in their hot opposition to his choice of an Ethiopian woman as his bride (Numbers 12:1)? From the little we know of Zipporah she does not seem to have had much kindly, home-making qualities. She would seem to have been a disrespectful wife. Was there a rift, and, if so, did the boys sense this? Were they perhaps alienated from the work in which they could have played such a leading role?

The Scriptures give us no answers. We are left to look for answers in our own homes, in our own hearts, in our own consciences. Do we fail in the home? Do we devote enough time to those whom God has entrusted to us? A busy father was once persuaded to spend a day with his son. At the end of the day he wrote in his diary: 'I spent the day with John; a totally wasted day.' Little John wrote in his diary: 'I spent the day with Daddy; the most wonderful day of my life.'

When the time came for Moses to put off the leadership, his eye was not dim nor had his strength abated. He was still able, but he had simply to stand aside for another to take his place in the ongoing plan of God. It would have been so much less painful to have handed it to his own sons than to another man. If only Gershom or Eliezer had been suitable and prepared to take the reins of leadership, it would have eased the pain of relinquishment. But now he had no son of his own to take his place and to finish his work. Instead, the Lord said to him, 'Take Joshua, the son of Nun … and lay your hand on him' (Numbers 27:18).

Joshua—successor to Moses

Joshua was born as a slave in Egypt (Numbers 32:11–12) of the tribe of Ephraim, the most powerful tribe at that time.

He and Caleb were the only two above twenty years of age to leave Egypt and enter Canaan. The others all died in the wilderness. Joshua was the son of Nun, the son of Elishama, who was the leader of the tribe of Ephraim (Numbers 1:10; 1 Chronicles 7:26–27). His life can be divided into three stages: firstly, as a slave in Egypt for about forty-five years, then in the wilderness under Moses' leadership for forty years, and finally as the leader of the conquering tribes in Canaan for about twenty-five years.

Joshua is presented as the successor to Moses (1:5; 3:7). He emulated Moses in several ways. Moses led Israel in the crossing of the Red Sea, and Joshua led Israel in the crossing of the Jordan. Moses had the experience of God speaking to him from the burning bush, and Joshua had the encounter with the Captain of the Lord's army. He repeated Moses' function as intercessor (7:6–9 and Deuteronomy 9:25–29). He held up his sword against the enemy, much as Moses held up his rod at the Red Sea (Exodus 14:16), and his arms in battle (8:18 and Exodus 17:11). Like Moses, Joshua sometimes spoke as a prophet (6:26; 7:13; 24:2). However, Joshua did not take over Moses' office as lawgiver, but constantly pointed back to the law which Moses gave.

Moses and Joshua as types

Moses bringing Israel out of Egypt typifies the Lord Jesus bringing his people out of this world which is under judgement; Moses the mediator and Aaron the high priest typify Jesus leading his people through this wilderness world. Joshua bringing Israel into Canaan typifies Christ, risen from the dead, leading his people into the land of victory and glory, and into conflict with the enemy in the heavenly places.

Moses the lawgiver could not lead the people into the land that signified the rich inheritance in Christ. He had to die so that Joshua, typifying our heavenly Joshua, the Lord Jesus, could lead them into that land. The law is our schoolmaster to bring us to Christ—then we are no longer under the law but under grace. Moses represents the law, but Joshua represents the Lord Jesus leading us into all the inheritance that we have in him. We are dead to the law but alive in Christ. He is our rich inheritance and our abundant possession.

A further facet of Moses the legislator is that Joshua was trained up under Moses and was fully committed to the law. When Moses died, Joshua emerged from this training to lead Israel. He is a picture of Jesus, who was under Moses, fully keeping the law and fulfilling all its righteousness: 'God sent forth his Son, born of a woman, born under the law' (Galatians 4:4). The law brought conviction: 'By the law is the knowledge of sin' (Romans 3:20); but Christ brought salvation: 'He has appeared to put away sin by the sacrifice of himself' (Hebrews 9:26). Jesus might well be called 'Moses' minister'—for he fulfilled the law— but then emerged to lead the church into a righteousness which is by faith.

Joshua's faithful service

Joshua's name was originally 'Hoshea', which Moses changed to 'Jehoshua' (Numbers 13:16), or, in its abbreviated form, 'Joshua'. Oshua means 'salvation', and Jehoshua, 'he by whom Jehovah will save'. In the

Greek, 'Joshua' is precisely the same as 'Jesus', i.e. 'Saviour' (Acts 7:45; Hebrews 4:8).

Joshua is introduced to us abruptly in Exodus 17:8–9, where he is commissioned by Moses to be the general and to fight the Amalekites, whom he decisively conquers. Obviously Moses had already assessed Joshua's worth as an energetic man of valour and an able leader. We read that Joshua did as Moses commanded him. He neither argued nor complained; he simply obeyed. If he was to lead the nation, he needed first of all to learn to take orders. From this first introduction to him we realize that learning to serve was a necessary part of his training. In this school of obedience he was prepared for leadership. He had to learn to obey before he was qualified to command. God normally gives us a period of apprenticeship before placing us in a position of authority.

In all those years of ministry to Moses, Joshua was faithful. It was behind the scenes that Joshua proved his worth. Then suddenly, after so many years of faithfulness, God commanded him to assume the position of leadership of this great people.

We too are to be faithful in every situation in which God places us. Who can tell what God is training us for? Sometimes our little sphere of service seems to be so insignificant and we may feel that we are fitted for something better. We may be in a place which seems to be leading nowhere and is very unimportant and, perhaps, unproductive. It is then that we are to see beyond the immediate and trust that God will accomplish his purpose in our lives. Let us not turn and seek another path when God is in the process of making us and preparing us for something of which we now know nothing. Remember that Jesus said to his disciples, 'Follow me, and I will make you become fishers of men' (Mark 1:17). When he is busy making us and preparing us, we must allow him to do it, even if at the time it seems to us to be obscure or unsuitable.

Remember too that Joshua was a type of Jesus, who put in thirty years of preparation. He was obedient to his parents, he knew the discipline of the home, he dignified hard work as a carpenter, he moved in a very narrow circle and he was not a prominent personality in the community. But one day, he stepped out of obscurity and entered into the greatest of all works—that of saving mankind. He patiently did the Father's will behind the scenes in the home of Joseph and Mary, and when the time was ripe, he was called to his mission.

Joshua's character revealed in history

THE AMALEKITES (EXODUS 17)

In Joshua's first command we also have a hint of his future work as an appointed instrument to execute judgement on God's enemies in the land of Canaan. It is as a warrior that Joshua first appears to us. His first battle, against the Amalekites, was fought and won not merely by physical effort but also on the basis of faith. It was a spiritual battle as well as a physical one, and indicated the realm in which Joshua was to move throughout his career. Joshua, as leader, went out to fight the Amalekites while Moses entered into the spiritual battle on the hill together with Aaron and Hur. They held up Moses' hands in an attitude of prayer, and, through the sword in the valley and prayer on the mountain, the battle was won. Joshua learned that *prayer is essential* in the battles of life, and he also learned that it is God who gives the victory. There is a sense in which this incident speaks of the use of the sword of the Spirit, the Bible, in our battles, of our need of one another in prayer, and also of our dependence on the intercessory prayers of our great High Priest.

ALONE ON THE MOUNTAIN (EXODUS 32)

Our next encounter with Joshua is when God gave the Ten Commandments to Moses on Mount Sinai. Here Joshua is called Moses' 'assistant' (Exodus 24:13), or minister, servant, supporter, colleague—an honoured position. When Moses left the camp to go up the mountain Joshua accompanied him, though apparently only part of the way. He was left alone for forty days and forty nights. Those in the camp, under Aaron's leadership, turned to idols, but Joshua remained true to his leader. This period of being alone must have been a great test to his faith, patience and fidelity, but he passed with flying colours. He perseveringly awaited the return of his master. He was learning *the value of quiet times with God*.

THE TENT OF MEETING (EXODUS 33)

He was placed in charge of the tabernacle when the idolatry of the people caused it to be moved outside the camp (Exodus 33:11). This was the prototype of the tabernacle which was yet to be built. The tabernacle was the most important thing in Israel and for him to be given charge of it indicated that Moses held him in the highest regard and trust. His position here is one of distinguished favour and is a recognition of his spiritual aspirations. He was learning that *communion with God is essential in God's work*.

PROPHESYING IN THE CAMP (NUMBERS 11)

Joshua proved his *loyalty* when he thought that the leadership was being threatened. When two of the elders, Eldad and Medad, prophesied in the camp, Joshua, in his zeal to protect his master's reputation and position, said to Moses, 'Moses my lord, forbid them!' He did not take it upon himself to rebuke the elders but recognized Moses' authority. There was no jealousy or self-seeking here, but only a concern for Moses' honour which Moses recognized in his reply: 'Are you zealous for my sake?' (Numbers 11:28–29). He was learning that *God works through whom he will*.

KADESH BARNEA (NUMBERS 13–14)

At Kadesh Barnea, Joshua was chosen to be the representative of his tribe, the tribe of Ephraim (Numbers 13:8,16) and he, together with eleven other leaders, was sent to spy out the land of Canaan before the invasion (v. 17).

Ten spies looked at the land from a natural viewpoint and saw that it would be altogether impossible for a company of slaves with neither weapons nor strategy to conquer the imposing walled cities with their strong inhabitants. Two, Joshua and Caleb, said that the Israelites were well able to overcome the land, for God was with them. It was a matter of faith in a God who was able to roll back the Red Sea, provide manna for at least two and a half million people in the wilderness, bring water from the rock, keep their shoes on their feet without wearing out and save them from their enemies. This God was sufficient for all that they had seen, and Israel should advance and conquer! 'Let us go up at once and take possession,' said Caleb, 'for we are well able to overcome it' (Numbers 13:30). Joshua was learning *the secret of faith in God.*

When the Israelites rebelled and exclaimed that they would make a captain for themselves and return to Egypt, Moses and Aaron fell on their faces and Joshua and Caleb tore their clothes. They said, 'Do not rebel against the LORD, nor fear the people of the land, for they are our bread; their protection has departed from them, and the LORD is with us. Do not fear them' (Numbers 14:8–9). Here we see their spiritual character and calibre, their confidence in God and their courage. Their faith in God was expressed in the face of national wrath and rebellion and they could have been killed, for the people wanted to 'stone them with stones'. Yet they stood firm in the midst of opposition. Joshua's life of faith in a leadership role had begun in the arena of the failing, faithless people of God.

No evil is recorded against Joshua. He did not selfishly desire personal advantage. There was no lust for selfish gain. His life was characterized by obedient faith, dauntless courage, indomitable perseverance and a total dedication to God and his word. He revealed cheerful confidence in the face of difficulties. Others gave him high honour because of his unselfish disregard of his own personal interests. He not only won battles and secured possession of the land, but he was also able to hold the people to perfect loyalty throughout his whole life (24:31). He was always concerned for the interests of those around him. In him God found a man who would *listen to instructions and who would complete his assignments.* In every circumstance he displayed a supreme desire to know the will of God, so when God needed a well-prepared man he found Joshua.

The land

In 1 Corinthians 10:11 we read, 'Now all these things happened to them as examples, and they were written for our admonition.' This includes, of course, the eternal example of the Israelites' journey from Egypt to Canaan, a wonderful picture and analogy of the Christian's redemption and journey through life.

They were saved from the cruel bondage in Egypt by the lambs' blood which was brushed by faith onto the doorposts. The firstborn lived because a lamb had died in his place. It was salvation by substitution. We too live because the Lamb of God died in our place. In Egypt we have the type of the One who came many years later to take our place.

The people then left Egypt. Salvation by blood meant separation from Egypt. So often today Christian folk carry so much of the Egypt of the old life around with them. In reality, although they may be out of Egypt, Egypt is not out of them. The line of demarcation is very thinly drawn. If you look for the church you will find it in the world, and if you look for the world you will find it in the church. There is an unwholesome mixture, weakening the witness and effectiveness of the church.

The people journeyed then for about a year and a half in the wilderness where they were given the constitution of the nation and instructed in godly living. There is a legitimate period when we journey with God in the wilderness and are established in grace. This is a time of early consolidation and instruction—yet we move on from the initial phase of teaching to full manhood.

The Israelites were then commanded to go up to possess the land which God had promised to Abraham. They journeyed from Sinai to Kadesh Barnea, from where the twelve spies surveyed the land of Canaan. On their return, ten stated that it was impossible to conquer the people of the land,

and two, Joshua and Caleb, firmly asserted that they were well able to overcome them. The people rebelled and refused to enter.

From that point of rebellion the Israelites wandered in the wilderness for another thirty-eight years. This was a tragic period in their history; all of those who left Egypt and were over the age of twenty (except Joshua and Caleb) died in the wilderness (Numbers 14:29). Forty years after they left Egypt, the new generation entered Canaan from the east by crossing the Jordan River. This epic journey from Egypt to Canaan holds great lessons of faith.

While in the wilderness, although they had been redeemed by blood, they were not in the place of their appointed inheritance, the place to which God had promised to take them. Because they did not believe that God could give them the land in the face of all the giants and walled cities, they died in the wilderness. Their incomprehensible lack of faith in and obedience to the One who had led them and fed them so miraculously through the great, howling wilderness, where there was neither food nor water, prevented their advancing and claiming that which God had intended for them.

Like them, through unbelief and disobedience we too can miss the wonderful fullness and the blessed nearness of the Lord Jesus, indwelling and enthroned, possessing, controlling and motivating our lives. We too can die in the wilderness of blighted hopes and unfulfilled aspirations, of inward battles and outward failures, of sad defeats and wasted years. How sad to hobble through life and end it without experiencing the mighty dynamic of the triumphant resurrected Lord, to live nowhere near the glory of the life hid in God and revealed in emphatic Christian victory! That weak, ineffective Christian life is most certainly not the inheritance which we have in Christ. Let us rise up and claim that which is rightfully ours in him.

Canaan not heaven in the first instance

Only in a lesser sense does Canaan represent heaven. Many are the hymns and Negro spirituals that are written about the rolling waters of Jordan (meaning death) being the last obstacle to Christians before they enter heaven. This is understandable and acceptable because it is the end of the journey, but it is not the primary meaning of the journey from Egypt to Canaan. The primary meaning is the fullness of life and of the Spirit, the rich and glorious heritage in Christ, 'the fullness of the blessing of the gospel of Christ' (Romans 15:29).

Graham Scroggie, in *The Land and Life of Rest*, says, 'What historically was the land of rest, spiritually is the life of rest. To the Israelites the sphere of rest was a place, but to us it is a Person, "in Christ in heavenly places" (Ephesians 1:3). Christ is our inheritance as Canaan was theirs.'[1] And again:

In these hymns the Jordan is taken to represent death, and Canaan to represent heaven. If that were so, heaven would lose much of its attractiveness for some of us, for to pursue the illustration, the first thing we would have to do on arriving would be to start a vigorous fight; and what is worse, if this representation were true, we would take into heaven all our faults and failings, to perpetuate there, what we bemoan here.[2]

Many commentators agree with Scroggie in this interpretation, among them: Oswald Smith, Alan Redpath, Warren Wiersbe, F. B. Meyer, J. Oswald Sanders, Andrew Murray, Sidlow Baxter, A. W. Pink and A. B. Simpson. These and many others would say with Sanders that Canaan 'stands for a victorious type of Christian experience that it is possible to know and enjoy here and now.'[3]

Paul speaks of 'the natural man' (the unsaved person), 'the carnal man' (the babes in Christ—Christians who are ruled by worldly values) and 'the spiritual man' (1 Corinthians 2:14–3:4). Andrew Murray, in *The Holiest of All*, says:

I cannot with too much earnestness urge every Christian reader to learn well the two stages of the Christian. There are the carnal, and there are the spiritual; there are those who remain babes, and those who are full-grown men. There are those who come up out of Egypt, but then remain in the wilderness of a worldly life; there are those who follow the Lord fully, and enter the life of rest and victory. Let each of us find out where we stand, and taking earnest heed to God's warnings, with our whole heart press on to go all the length in following Jesus, in seeking to stand perfect and complete in all the will of God.4

There are four reasons why Canaan should not be regarded in its primary objective as heaven:

- The Israelites had their biggest battles in Canaan. When we get to heaven there will be no more battles and no more defeats.
- The Bible teaches that nothing that defiles can enter heaven, but Israel sinned grievously in Canaan.
- They were dispossessed of Canaan. In 722 BC the Assyrians led the Northern Kingdom of Israel away captive, and in 606, 597 and 586 BC Babylonians destroyed the Southern Kingdom of Judah and carried them away into captivity for seventy years. When we get to heaven there will be no possibility of being expelled.
- The exhortations in Hebrews chapters 3 and 4 indicate that we are to strive to enter into the land of rest: 'They could not enter in because of unbelief. Therefore, since a promise remains of entering his rest, let us fear lest any of you seem to have come short of it' (Hebrews 3:19; 4:1); 'There remains therefore a rest for the people of God' (4:9); 'For we who have believed do enter that rest' (4:3); 'Let us therefore be diligent to enter that rest, lest anyone fall according to the same example of disobedience' (4:11). These passages clearly indicate that it is for us to acknowledge that there is such a thing as an experience of 'rest' for the children of God here and now, and that we should go after it with diligence.

Paul speaks of the natural, carnal and spiritual (1 Corinthians 2:14–3:3).

The counterparts in type are Egypt, the wilderness and Canaan, respectively. We left the natural when we came out of Egypt, and we leave the carnal when we come out of the wilderness and enter the Canaan-land of rest.

Canaan—a type of the life of the fullness of blessing

IT WAS A DWELLING-PLACE (JOSHUA 1:2–9)

The Israelites had no permanent dwelling-place after crossing the Red Sea. They were now being drawn by the prospects of the fertile land that lay ahead. Soon they were to be established in a land where they would live in permanent houses.

After experiences of defeat and inconsistent wandering spiritually, we come to a place of established blessing in which we find a stable relationship with the Lord.

IT WAS A PLACE OF REST (JOSHUA 1:2–9)

They were to have rest from weary wanderings, deviations, doubts, defeats, murmurings, hungering and thirsting. All these are there in the wilderness of carnality. We find that the civil war within our own hearts continues to rob us of our joy and our fellowship with the Lord. Indeed, because of the carnality surging in our hearts, bringing self-reproach, we sometimes almost despair of ever coming to a place of victory and deliverance. But 'there remains … a rest for the people of God … Let us therefore be diligent to enter that rest.'

IT WAS A GOOD LAND (DEUTERONOMY 8:7)

The land was desirable in location, and good for health and fruitfulness. At last they would be able to establish normal relationships with permanent neighbours. It would be good for their children, for their families, for their communities, for mutual aid, for the development of skills, for trade and expansion. It was a good land.

Holiness is good for the soul. When conflict has ceased and the soul is at rest, development is quicker than ever before. Living in the full blessing of the Lord gives ease in relationships; it enables us to bear and forbear, to forgive and to live together more harmoniously than before. It is a good land to which the Lord is leading us.

IT WAS A WATERED LAND (DEUTERONOMY 8:7)

It was 'a land of brooks of water, of fountains and springs, that flow out of valleys and hills'.

Jesus said, 'If anyone thirsts, let him come to me and drink. He who believes in me, as the Scripture has said, out of his heart will flow rivers of living water' (John 7:37–38). Faith is connected to usefulness. From those who find their full satisfaction in Jesus will flow rivers of blessing.

IT WAS A FRUITFUL LAND (DEUTERONOMY 8:8–9)

It was 'a land of wheat and barley, of vines and fig trees and pomegranates, a land of olive oil and honey; a land in which you will eat bread without scarcity, in which you will lack nothing'. It was a land of plenty and sufficiency.

'I am the bread of life', and 'I am the vine', said Jesus. We now live in him and from him have our 'fruit to holiness' (Romans 6:22).

Furthermore, it was a land of oil, a picture of the Holy Spirit. That heavenly anointing is the portion and privilege of those who dwell in the land which fills us with good things. 'You have an anointing from the Holy One' (1 John 2:20,27).

It was also the land of honey. Sour holiness is sham holiness, but there is a beautiful sweetness, a loveliness, an unconscious spiritual quality which rests upon the one who is in love with the Saviour.

IT WAS A LAND OF STRENGTH AND STABILITY (DEUTERONOMY 8:9)

It was 'a land whose stones are iron and out of whose hills you can dig copper'. Metal could be extracted for industry and progress. Resources were there which were sufficient to meet all their developing needs. There was something very solid and lasting in this land, something which would not be blown away by winds of adversity. Iron and copper were there to be found and dug out to be used to the best advantage.

As we dig into the Word we will be established all the more firmly in the truths of the gospel.

IT WAS A LAND SPECIALLY CARED FOR (DEUTERONOMY 11:12)

It was 'a land for which the LORD your God cares'. 'For the eyes of the LORD run to and fro throughout the whole earth, to show himself strong on behalf of those whose heart is loyal to him' (2 Chronicles 16:9). 'He cares for you' (1 Peter 5:7).

The Lord guides us in our perplexities; strengthens us in our weakness; comforts us in our sorrows; enables us in our duties; empowers us in our ministries. He understands our innermost needs and tenderly sorts out our problems; he loves us in spite of what we are. We serve him with deep gratitude. 'We love him because he first loved us' (1 John 4:19).

IT WAS A LAND TO BE POSSESSED (JOSHUA 1:3)

'Every place that the sole of your foot will tread upon I have given you, as I said to Moses.' We can have all we can take! This is a matter of faith and obedience. We must claim by faith all that God gives us in Christ. For the Israelites, much heavy fighting lay ahead. Seven nations held the land of Canaan (3:10), and to conquer and possess it was a huge undertaking.

The land of the fullness of the blessing of Christ is certainly not free from the presence of foes. Each step forward will be contested. But Jesus has conquered the forces of evil and Satan is a defeated foe. The rich inheritance in Christ is being given to us. If we turn aside from the wonderful offer of God, we shall die in the wilderness of unbelief and disobedience. Go up at once and take what God is giving.

In summary, this land may be described as having various qualities:

- It is a land of *reality*. It is not all hope and make-believe. It brings us to a real experience of grace and power.
- It is a land of *tranquillity*. It is rest in the living God who gives peace that passes all understanding—and all misunderstanding, as well. It is a supernatural calm in the midst of things that would normally drive one crazy.
- It is a land of *victory*. There is triumph in the hard places. Don't think that difficulties cannot be overcome. There is a life of victory for you!
- It is a land of *fecundity*. There is fruitfulness. We read of the grapes of Eschol (Numbers 13:23) in Galatians 5:22—the fruit of the Spirit. The love, joy, peace, etc., are now in evidence in their abundance. If we are part of the vine they cannot help growing upon us.
- It is a land of *opportunity*. Each has his or her own inheritance. They were allotted their special places in Canaan. Don't miss what God has for you. Whatever your foot treads upon is yours, so start walking! There is much land to be possessed. There are great opportunities in grace.
- It is a land of *community*. The more you advance in the life of the Spirit, the more others will profit from your dedication and faith. The closer you get to God, the closer you will be to those who love him, too. Fellowship is sweet.
- It is a land of *proximity*. It is not far away. Caleb said, 'Let us go up at once and take possession' (Numbers 13:30), and again, 'Give me this mountain' (Joshua 14:12). We don't have to wait years to enter into the land—it is before us! We must just go forward and possess it as we trust in the living God to lead us on to victory.

'Lord, give us the vision, faith, obedience, dedication and determination of Joshua and Caleb, who went forward at your command in spite of difficulties, and saw your mighty hand at work because they trusted you.'

Chapter 3

Notes

1 **Graham Scroggie,** *The Land and Life of Rest* (London: Pickering & Inglis, 1950), p. 9.
2 Ibid. p. 17.
3 **J. Oswald Sanders,** *The Christian's Promised Land* (Eastbourne: Kingsway, 1984), p. 35.
4 **Andrew Murray,** *The Holiest of All* (London: Marshall, Morgan & Scott, 1976), p. 141.

Why they did not enter the land

The twelve spies had returned and had given their reports. It seemed madness to continue with this apparently ill-fated venture, for ten of the spies said emphatically, 'We are not able to go up against the people, for they are stronger than we' (Numbers 13:31). Only Joshua and Caleb declared that 'we are well able to overcome it' and urged the people not to rebel, saying 'the LORD is with us' (Numbers 14:9).

'All the congregation lifted up their voices and cried, and the people wept that night. And … the whole congregation said … 'Let us select a leader and return to Egypt' (Numbers 14:1–2,4). God was angry and would have destroyed them but for the intercessions of Moses. God answered Moses' plea and pardoned them, but declared that 'in this wilderness … they shall die' (Numbers 14:35).

This whole story is graphically related to us in Hebrews chapters 3 and 4, where the clear evidence against the Israelites builds up to show that the reason they did not enter the land was because of *unbelief* and *disobedience*.

They did not believe because of what they saw

The spies reported: 'The people who dwell in the land are strong; the cities are fortified and very large; moreover we saw the descendants of Anak there … The land … devours its inhabitants, and all the people whom we saw in it are men of great stature. There we saw the giants … and we were like grasshoppers in our own sight, and so we were in their sight' (Numbers 13:28,32–33).

They saw the giants! It was impossible to conquer the giants! Oh, those awesome and intimidating giants! There was no way by which they could overcome them. The people could not believe that they had been led into such a trap. They were infuriated. 'All the congregation said to stone them with stones' (Numbers 14:10). 'Let's go back to Egypt' was their only thought.

Ah, the giants! How they stand unassailable in their fortresses, awesome in their strength. Who could conquer the giants?

Do you know anything about the giants? The giants which intimidate and prevent any thought of your being able to inherit the land of the spiritual riches in Christ? You have come a long way through all sorts of experiences in life. You have been born again and have known God's presence and blessing, but now, when faced with the possibilities of victory, even when you are exhorted to enter the land of plenty by the Word of God, by the servants of God, by the Spirit of God within you, you stand unbelievingly aside and say, 'It is impossible.'

You see yourself as but a grasshopper in the face of these powerful giants. You have increased your praying, your reading of the Bible, your earnestness; but those qualities which you know to be yours in Christ seem to evade you. You try to keep your temper under control but there are those moments …! And the critical and sometimes lustful thoughts which plague your mind—the wild imaginings! Self-pity and bitterness at times invade the scene. Then remorse sets in and you come before God in tears.

This land may be for some people, but it seems it's not for you! Living as you know you should and revealing a Christ-like spirit seems just out of your reach. Sometimes there is such joy as you serve him and as you mix happily with others, but when the clash of wills takes place there is inward turmoil and an inexplicable lack of ability to rise above that which damages your spirit. There are giants!

You had thought that by coming to Christ your problems would be solved and that you would be relieved of so much burden and blame. True, the burden of guilt vanished and you entered into a wonderful new life with God. You were saved and you knew it. Your life had been transformed, but now you realize that there is something else within you that gives expression to its awesome power and makes you wonder at times just how much you have been changed. Not even those closest to you know the inward battles you go through. There seems to be a continual and irreconcilable war. The eruptions of inward corruption and the outbursts of evil temper spoil the testimony to the saving work of Christ. Others see it and wonder. You try to be as sweet and as Christ-like as you can be, but it does not always work. The struggle is real and the battle fierce. What can you do? The giants seem so secure in their impregnable fortresses. They will never be conquered.

The harsh, irritable words spoken to those who live with you are painfully embarrassing. You sometimes seem to be a cantankerous beast. The worst seems to come out of you at home when all the defences are down and your family sees you as you really are. Oh, at the church they know you as a pleasant and happy Christian, but they know nothing! You just keep up appearances, and it seems that all is well. But all is not well!

You can be so touchy and sensitive about things. Just a little word spoken in jest, or even a chance remark sets you off on a line of sullen moodiness. You get the sulks. The great Number One has been offended. 'What's wrong?' they ask. 'No, nothing's wrong'—but you are writhing inside.

And what about vanity, envy, jealousy and pride? The inordinate amount of time that you spend on yourself for appearance's sake? There is pride of lace, of place, of race, of grace. Even our pride can be hidden by a veneer of seeming humility. How jealous you can be of all sorts of things and people. Their position grieves you; why should they have that position when you are far more capable? Why should he be asked to preach when I can do a far better job? Why do they flock to her or him for counsel when I am better trained and could give better advice? You are consumed with envy and jealousy. The feelings come out in snide remarks, undercover whisperings, hurtful accusations. Malice is not in short supply. It damages the fellowship, and relationships are marred. All because of uncrucified flesh, of the giants within.

What of the whole area of impurity? Nobody knows what you are thinking and nobody can expose all the fantasies, imaginations and evil thoughts that tour your mind and sometimes settle and gather to explode like a mighty volcano of lust and desire.

Then it must all be covered up. No one must know of these failures, these giants. You are supposed to be a respectable and honourable Christian in the fellowship and community, so you smile and shake hands enthusiastically, and laugh, and pray in the prayer meeting, and testify to the Lord's goodness. And that is very real and wonderful. Why can't it be like that all the time? It seems so hypocritical to keep covering up all these undesirable qualities! When will you face the truth? You have a huge problem. By some inconceivably merciful blow—and sometimes it's a humiliating one—God sometimes forces it all out into the open. You see yourself as you really are, and know that you need the help of the Lord to conquer the giants and to enter the land of plenty and eat its pleasant fruits.

Long ago, a farmer-preacher called Archie Gush was ploughing with his oxen in a field. At the end of the field the oxen would turn and begin the next furrow. Once, they turned the wrong way and Archie lost his temper. He shouted and kicked the oxen, forcing them into the right way once again. As they began that next furrow, Archie suddenly realized what had happened. He left the oxen right there in the field and went to a tree at the edge of the field. There he knelt and cried to God, not only for forgiveness for what had happened, but also for deliverance from that which had brought such defeat into his life. God met him under the tree at the side of that field and he testified far and wide to God's wonderful salvation which reached him in his great need. We do not need to go throughout our lives bent under the terrible burden of soul-destroying defeat, for in Jesus Christ is the answer to the problem of the giants which may at the moment so dominate and spoil life.

God had pledged to save the people from the hand of the enemy, yet they refused to move. The writer to the Hebrews calls it the 'evil heart of unbelief' (Hebrews 3:12).

They did not believe because of what they heard

Ten spies returned with the news that, after experiencing such difficulties in their many journeys, it was altogether impossible to conquer the land. Only two recommended advance. What a test! The report from the ten was so convincing that the people revolted and turned back into the wilderness. What a tragedy!

People come from different spiritual backgrounds and consequently express themselves differently. Some would speak of 'entire consecration', others of 'the life [or rest] of faith', others of 'being filled with the Spirit', and others of 'the sanctifying grace of God'. The descriptions of their experiences and their expositions of the Scriptures vary in accordance with their training and spiritual upbringing. Augustine said long ago that 'no single group has all the truth'. As long as men have different ways of looking at things, and have different degrees of light, they are bound to differ in their explanations of the theory of walking with God. We look through a glass darkly, or 'we see in a mirror dimly' (1 Corinthians 13:12). It is not to be expected that all men should agree in theory as regards these truths, but there should be a practical agreement concerning the actual knowledge and experience of the life of holiness and fullness.

Surely the main thing is to walk with God and to seek him with all the heart; to preach a total commitment and dedication to the One to whom we owe our full allegiance. Half-heartedness and shallow Christian living is to be shunned, and all who are well-taught in the Word, whatever particular brand of theological emphasis they may have, recognize that this is the message which must be preached to the many who live worldly, self-centred Christian lives.

When someone testifies with a burning heart to what God has done for him or her, and claims that such intimacy and victory is for others as well, he or she can sometimes be ridiculed as being over-enthusiastic or even an extremist. So many are in the carnal bracket and say with a smirk, 'we're human and we are all sinners'. Excuses are made for unacceptable carnality.

Many have been living in a half-hearted, lukewarm condition for so long that they deny that folk *can* walk with God in a way which glorifies him. In fact, so much of the church is in a worldly, unseparated state that the message of fullness, holiness and victory is a foreign language. They are content with their meagre experience, for it allows them to indulge in questionable amusements and practices while retaining a veneer of respectability and religion. Andrew Murray says, 'With the Reformation the great truth of Justification, the bringing out from the bondage of Egypt, is restored to its place. But the other great truth of Sanctification, the bringing in into the land with its rest and victory, has never yet taken the place in the preaching and practice of the Church which God's Word claims for it.'[1]

The problem is that, because so many have such a low standard, they shrug off the need to go deeper and reach higher. And preachers, too, realize that if they were to present the strong demands of the gospel in the realm of holiness, they would create opposition for themselves. If able people were offended, what would become of the church income? These are all reasons to tone down the message. So, when the preachers don't require it, the people don't expect it. If they hear that this matter is obligatory, they refuse any urgent preaching in the realm of holiness and victory, speaking of it as impractical and impossible. In fact, it is the voice of the majority which we hear refusing the requirements and blessing of absolute surrender, heart holiness and the fullness of the blessing of Christ.

It was also the voice of the majority to which the Israelites listened and yielded. They could not conceive of conquering a land which was so full of awesome giants and reinforced strongholds. Ten spies confirmed that it was impossible and only two contradicted them. The voice of the majority prevailed. The multitude believed them and turned around to continue their wilderness experience. The voice of the majority so often has enormous weight; and it frequently carries the day.

But there are those who have discovered the secret of a life hid with Christ in God. Don't pass them by. Don't turn away as if it were all an impossible dream. Don't think this to be merely an eternal approximation to an unrealizable ideal. Don't think that this intimate, holy life of fellowship with God is but for a limited few who may have time for such matters. Don't think that this is just for preachers and Christian workers. Don't give in to the majority voice, otherwise you too will tragically have to backtrack into the wilderness, and perhaps you too will die there. Listen to those two spies who said, 'Let us go up at once and take possession ... the LORD is with us' (Numbers 13:30; 14:9). Surely he has brought us this far and will not leave us now to sink in despair at not being able to conquer the giants nor possess the land of rest. This is our inheritance in Christ.

They did not believe because of what they forgot

THEY FORGOT THE PURPOSE OF GOD

'He brought us out from there, that he might bring us in, to give us the land of which he swore to our fathers' (Deuteronomy 6:23). That was the reason they left Egypt. Out of the bondage of Egypt they journeyed to a land which God would give them. The objective was ever held before them. It was the reason why they were in the wilderness. This was an intermediate state and they were on a journey to the Land.

THEY FORGOT THE POWER OF GOD

They had seen what God had done in Egypt. They were eyewitnesses to it all. The firstborn of the nation were alive because they had obeyed God's command and placed the blood on the doorposts. There were many firstborn in that company who refused to enter. They had seen what God did at the Red Sea only two years before. They had witnessed the power of Almighty God rolling back the waters. Now when that same God tells them to enter the land and that he will deal with the giants, they cannot believe him.

Do we not remember those wonderful days when we came to Jesus and found him to be a mighty Saviour who forgave us all our sins and who came to live within us? Yes, we knew the power of God! And now when he says, 'Go up and possess the land of rest', we do not believe him. He cannot deal with the giants in our lives.

THEY FORGOT THE PRESENCE OF GOD

'Out of heaven he let you hear his voice, that he might instruct you … you heard his words out of the midst of the fire' (Deuteronomy 4:36). All they had to do to find out if God was still with them was to lift the flap of their tent. There in the centre of the camp rose the column of smoke by day and the fiery pillar by night. The Lord was still in the midst of his people! What comfort and confidence that brought them.

Has the Lord not been with us again and again? Have we not sensed his presence chastening, guiding, bringing us such joy, warming our hearts and sometimes breaking them so that the tears flowed freely? Perhaps we too say in unbelief, 'No, Lord, the giants are too big and strong. They cannot be conquered, and I cannot believe that I can be rid of them. I don't think that I can be delivered and live victoriously. It's no good even trying.'

THEY FORGOT THE PROTECTION OF GOD

They were protected from disease, from wild animals and from their enemies. God cared for them and brought them through the wilderness. God has protected us physically, spiritually and in so many practical ways, yet we disbelieve him! The God who has proved stronger than all the forces arrayed against us is with us. No, we cannot doubt his power. His word stands. He will give us the victory—he has said so!

THEY FORGOT THE PROVISION OF GOD

How does one keep alive over two million people in a desert where no food can be produced and in which no water flows? It is an impossibility! But God did it! Water for all these people and their flocks and herds flowed from the stricken rock. Manna fell nightly all around the camp for them to pick up and eat—and there was always enough. Their shoes did not wear out. These things are simply unbelievable—yet they happened. God is a God of mighty power and he alone could have done these wonderful things. But there were giants—even this mighty God could not deal with the giants!

'Please, Lord, forgive us for not believing that you can deal with the most impossible things in our lives. We don't want to stand in unbelief and go back into the wilderness, when you are waiting to lead us on to the wonderful rest of God.'

THEY FORGOT THE PROMISES OF GOD

When they were in Egypt, God said to them, 'I am the LORD your God who brings you out from under the burdens of the Egyptians. And I will bring you into the land which I swore to give to Abraham, Isaac, and Jacob; and I will give it to you as a heritage' (Exodus 6:7–8). Just before the spies entered the land he said to them, 'Spy out the land of Canaan, which I am giving to the children of Israel' (Numbers 13:2).

What promises God has given us! 'But thanks be to God, who gives us the victory through our Lord Jesus Christ' (1 Corinthians 15:57). 'Now thanks be to God who always leads us in triumph in Christ, and through us diffuses the fragrance of his knowledge in every place' (2 Corinthians 2:14). 'And God is able to make all grace abound toward you, that you, always having all sufficiency in all things, may have an abundance for every good work' (2 Corinthians 9:8). 'Where sin abounded, grace abounded much more' (Romans 5:20). 'For sin shall not have dominion over you' (Romans 6:14). '... to know the love of Christ which passes knowledge; that you may be filled with all the fullness of God. Now to him who is able to do exceedingly abundantly above all that we ask or think ...' (Ephesians 3:19–20).

Are the promises not there to be claimed, to be possessed, to be made part of us? Is that not what happened when we first came to Christ? We believed the promise and our lives were transformed.

'As many as received him, to them he gave the right to become children of God' (John 1:12). We believed that word, received him by faith and we were born of the Spirit in the instant that we trusted. The promise was sufficient, and, because we trusted its truth and believed the One who made it, we received, by his grace, eternal life. The mighty word of God was effective in those who believed.

What now of *these* promises? Are they to lie unclaimed? They are there for the taking. Who will believe them, or rather, who will believe the God who made them? Surely if we do not believe what he says to us, we are casting doubt on his character. If God has said that sin will not have dominion over me and I do not believe that it is possible, then I am casting aspersions on the truthfulness and character of the God who made that promise to me. Unbelief is an evil thing. Come, let us trust the Lord who calls us through his Word and by his Spirit to a rich inheritance in Christ, to a life of rest and overcoming grace, to precious communion with him.

They did not believe because of what they did not realize

THERE WOULD BE FREEDOM INSTEAD OF SLAVERY

They well knew the harsh treatment meted out to them in Egypt. They knew what it was to be unfairly treated and punished for not fulfilling unreasonable demands. But ahead lay complete freedom. The soul of man longs to be free. It is one of the basic instincts in man, and now, just a little way ahead, lay freedom for these people. What fools to retreat at this crucial moment when that which they so deeply desired lay almost within their grasp! Incomprehensibly they turned from that immense prize and chose to return to the bondage from which they had thought they were free; all because they did not believe God.

THERE WOULD BE REST INSTEAD OF ANXIOUS WANDERING

For two years they had endured the fierce winds, the blinding heat and the weary wanderings of desert existence. Now God was offering them permanent homes. They were to go into the land to stay! Neighbourhood friendships and stable societies would develop.

No longer do we need to wander; we are at home base. We find the stability in Jesus Christ. Our wilderness wanderings are coming to a close and we are at home in him together with those who know the rest and the establishing blessing of the all-conquering Lord. This, to Hudson Taylor, was the greatest realization of the victorious life. He says, 'The sweetest part, if one may speak of one part being sweeter than another, is the rest which full identification with Christ brings.'2 Rest from an uneasy conscience, from the tyranny of sinful dominance, from the constant war with ungovernable selfish attitudes, from struggling so hard in my own strength to obtain a victory which just seems to elude my grasp. As I dare to trust him, he brings his own wonderful liberation to my poor heart and I rejoice in his wonderful and full salvation. Andrew Murray says, 'Trust Jesus, who through the sprinkling of the blood, brought you out of Egypt, to bring you as definitely into the rest ... Trust Jesus. Give up and forsake the wilderness. Follow him fully: he is the rest ... Yield thyself, in the death to self, to the will of God; have faith in Jesus on the throne, as thy Head and life, that he has brought thee in and will make it true in thy experience; trust Jesus, as being partaker of his nature and life, to work all in thee that the Father seeks; and thou shalt know how blessed it is to enter the rest of God.'3

THERE WOULD BE ABUNDANCE INSTEAD OF SHORTAGE AND DEARTH

The fields were arable and the crops would yield their increase. They would have wheat, barley, corn, figs, vineyards, cattle and sheep. There would be a marvellous sufficiency. There was no comparison to the sparse provisions of the desert. But no, there were giants there and it was impossible to occupy the land because the giants still reigned and exerted their influence.

Oh, how we find such riches in the One who is the Land and who gives us of his pleasant fruits and feeds us with food convenient for us! May God give us to know more of his grace and love as we trust him to reveal himself to us.

THERE WOULD BE VICTORY INSTEAD OF DEFEAT

They were expecting defeat at the hands of the giants, but God was offering them victory. No one would stand before them. Yet the promises of God were simply vague and distant to them, for they were looking straight at the powerful giants. God could not deliver them in these circumstances.

Don't look at the problems, however great those may be; look beyond the problems to the God who made the promises and whose word cannot be broken. He is worthy of being trusted!

Maybe we are at Kadesh Barnea—what a place! A place of opportunity, of faith for those few who trusted, of failure for the many who did not, of judgement upon the unbelievers and disobedient; a place of huge potential—lost forever.

'Therefore, since a promise remains of entering his rest, let us fear lest any of you seem to have come short of it' (Hebrews 4:1).

'Please, God, don't let me fail, but let me trust in the promises and inherit all the riches in the Lord Jesus.'

Notes

1   **Andrew Murray,** *The State of the Church* (London: James Nisbet & Co., n.d.), p. 69.

2   **J. Hudson Taylor,** quoted in **Colin N. Peckham,** *From Defeat to Victory* (Edinburgh: Faith Mission, 1993), pp. 4–5.

3   **Murray,** *The Holiest of All*, pp. 146, 150.

The preparation (1:1–18)

'Moses my servant is dead' (1:2)

W hat a shattering statement! Moses was gone! Suddenly the scene had changed, and when Israel needed him most, he was not there. He was no longer to be their commander when they were to face the might of the nations of Canaan. The timing seemed so inappropriate, but it was God's time. It was a painful loss and a severe test of their faith. They felt it keenly: 'And the children of Israel wept for Moses in the plains of Moab thirty days' (Deuteronomy 34:8).

We need to be reminded that the work of God will go on no matter who is removed. The work of the Kingdom is greater than any individual in that Kingdom. If God sees fit to remove one servant, he will send another. In fact, he is training new leaders even while the old ones are still in position. It is his work and he is in control. However acute and painful the loss may be, the Lord is never taken by surprise and works all things together for good to those who love him.

Moses had gone, but God had a man ready to take his place. Joshua had long been groomed for the job.

Joshua's selection (Numbers 27:18–23)
HE WAS CHOSEN (V. 18)
Joshua was God's choice, for God said to Moses, 'Take Joshua the son of Nun with you, a man in whom is the Spirit, and lay your hand on him' (v. 18). Joshua had proved himself over the years and now the time had come for action.

We cannot thrust ourselves into the work of God. 'No man takes this honour to himself, but he who is called by God' (Hebrews 5:4). It is only when the compulsion becomes overwhelming that we should move forward into the front line of his work.

Jesus himself was very conscious of being sent: 'My food is to do the will of him who sent me, and to finish his work' (John 4:34); 'As the Father has sent me, I also send you' (John 20:21). He was sent by the Father to do his will.

Jesus prayed all night before choosing his twelve disciples (Luke 6:12–13). He selected them from all the others who were following him. 'He appointed twelve, that they might be with him and that he might send them out to preach' (Mark 3:14). He said, 'You did not choose me, but I chose you and appointed you' (John 15:16).

Moses received a very definite charge from God which he did not want to pursue, but God prevailed and Moses went.

Gideon was very fearful, but God chose him and sent him.

The word of the Lord came to Jeremiah, saying, 'I ordained you a prophet to the nations' (Jeremiah 1:5), and despite his feelings of inadequacy and youthfulness, he obeyed and went. Of Paul we read, 'He is a chosen vessel of mine to bear my name before Gentiles' (Acts 9:15). The moment came when God arrested this savage oppressor, transformed him and sent him out to preach. God is sovereign in his choice of the messenger. He appoints whomever he wishes.

God needs men and women from all strata of society to reach all the different levels and cultures of people in so many places all over the world. He chooses, prepares and sends. The call of God is his enabling; it is a distinct qualification for leadership and an enormous source of strength. 'A man assured of the call of God is invincible,' said Alan Redpath.[1] To the one called by God, God says, 'I am with you always' (Matthew 28:20); and if the Almighty God is with us, who can be against us (Romans 8:31)? The supreme question is not: 'Are we qualified?' but 'Are we called?' If God calls us he will make us into that new, sharp threshing instrument which will thresh the mountains. Should a river stand in the way, we will go through it; should there be walled cities hindering our path, we will attack and conquer them. 'By you I can run against a troop, by my God I can leap over a wall' (Psalm 18:29). 'I can do all things through Christ who strengthens me' (Philippians 4:13).

Where did Jesus get the strength and stamina to go steadfastly towards Jerusalem to what he knew was an unthinkable end? 'For I have come … not to do my own will, but the will of him who sent me' (John 6:38); 'I delight to do your will, O my God' (Psalm 40:8). That's it! Sent! God is with me; God is enabling me; God opens closed doors. I move forward with God. Nothing is impossible with him.

HE WAS COMMISSIONED (VV. 19,22)

'Set him before Eleazar the priest and before all the congregation and inaugurate him in their sight.' He was set before Eleazar and before all Israel to be confirmed as their new leader.

The church needs to be involved actively in the acceptance and confirming of the missionary candidate or Christian leader. Sadly, many churches are led by those who do not see the point of missionary work at all. In such situations the whole biblical method of the church sending forth their missionaries, evangelists or pastors fails, and the individual must obey the leading of the Lord independently of those who should be supporting him or her but who are indifferent to the whole cause. In Joshua's case, however, the whole congregation was involved in the endorsement of him as their new leader.

Notice that it was the church at Jerusalem which 'sent out Barnabas to go as far as Antioch' to investigate the preaching of the gospel there (Acts 11:22). When Paul and Barnabas left the church at Antioch on their first missionary journey, it was a group decision, and they were sent out with the church's blessing (Acts 13:1–3). Later, Paul wanted to take Timothy with him on his journeys, for 'he was well spoken of by the brethren' (Acts 16:2). Paul's good choice was acceptable to the church and Timothy was on his way. Both the church and Paul recognized the qualities of the one who had been selected.

How good it is to have a congregation with one heart, one spirit and one vision for the salvation of the lost! They are then able to give their enthusiastic endorsement to those whom they acknowledge to be called of God and whom they can support by prayer and practical giving. It unites the worker and the congregation, and together they harvest souls for Christ through the labours of the commissioned candidate.

HE WAS CHARGED (V. 21)

He was to stand before Eleazar the priest to receive guidance from God. His charge was firstly a spiritual one. He was not to lean on his own understanding, but to get his instructions from God.

He was then to communicate those instructions, and he and all the congregation were to obey what God said. He was to be a mediator between God and his people, taking the lead and calling upon them to obey and do what God required. It was a very responsible position, for he had to be sure of what God was saying. He was to have a word from God for the people.

How *we* need to have a word from God for the people! How we need to live so close to our great High Priest in order to hear his slightest whisper and be able to give that word to the people! There are so many good theological words, ethical words, helpful words, but oh, for a word from God which stirs the soul and moves us Godwards! May God make us those leaders who will, above all else, be able to hear God speaking and be ready to communicate that message to those about us.

Joshua's motivation

He is motivated and encouraged by God, by Moses and by the people.

MOTIVATED BY GOD (JOSHUA 1:9)

'Have I not commanded you? Be strong and of good courage; do not be afraid, nor be dismayed, for the LORD your God is with you wherever you go.'

We see here:

The person of God

He is with you! He who wrought wonders in Egypt, who opened the Red Sea and brought the Israelites out of Egypt—this mighty God is with you! He was sufficient for the Israelites and he is sufficient for us. *God* is with us.

He uses the term *Yahweh* here wherever we have 'LORD' written in capitals; the name *Yahweh* means 'the self-existent One, the eternal I AM'.

This also signifies a continuing self-revelation. It therefore means 'the self-existent One who reveals himself'.

It is also distinctly the redemption name of deity, for the first revelation of himself by his name *Yahweh* (Jehovah) was in connection with the redemption of Israel from Egypt (Exodus 3:13–17).

It is also the distinctive name of deity in covenant with Israel (Exodus 19:3; 20:1–2; Jeremiah 31:31–34). God promised Abraham that he would give him and his descendants this land.

So this God—*Yahweh*—is the God who keeps his covenants, who reveals himself and who redeems his people.

To us today he is the great Redeemer from sin who keeps his covenants and has promised to forgive, cleanse and keep all those who place their trust in him. We can safely trust him to do what he has promised. He is also the One who continues to reveal himself as a wonderful Saviour. He is 'the self-existent One who reveals himself'. We keep getting fresh glimpses and manifestations of the One whom we love and serve. 'The LORD is with you.'

The promise of God

'The LORD your God *is* with you.' Why, this fact is certain—he *is* with us! We don't need to question whether it really be possible that, while God might be with so-and-so, who is so greatly used, he could also be with me in my little world. We are not alone, for he, the mighty God, is with us, and what he has promised, he will perform.

Not only is the promise certain, it is also given in the present tense: He is with us *now*! We can rely on his presence *now*. Do we need grace just now? He is the fountain of grace. Do we need strength in the face of fierce temptation? He is there to give us that strength. Do we need love for someone who has been anything but loving towards us? God is love. Do we need purity in the midst of an unclean world? God is holy and he is with us right now. It is a present-tense salvation. We can draw by faith upon the One who is with us and who possesses all the qualities in himself that we need at this moment. 'The LORD *is* with you.'

The presence of God

'The LORD your God is *with you*.' Joshua certainly wondered what the future held for him when he received the commission. What a moment it was! He was to lead Israel into the land and he needed all the guidance, wisdom, courage, tenacity, determination, tact, ability and every other quality that could be mustered for this enormous task. Then God says to him, 'I am with you.' His sufficiency is in God! What an inspiration, and what an encouragement! God is with me!

When we are confronted with tasks which are altogether too big for us, it is wonderful to have that secret whispered into our hearts: 'I am with you.' We discover that God is big enough to accomplish in and through us that to which he is calling us. My service is centred in him. In him I live and move and have my being, and in him I find an all-sufficient Lord.

When exhausted and strained, we can become disheartened and frustrated. We may feel overwhelmed, undervalued and unappreciated. We may fear that we will not be up to the next challenge. We may be caught up in spiritual depression and feel that this life of faith is too hard-going.

Then it is the presence of God, stealing into our hearts as we break through the barriers of disappointment and lethargy, that does it all. He brings his precious comfort and restores my soul. I draw upon his vast resources as I bow down at his feet and adore him. How indescribably precious and soothing are those moments when he comes near and reveals himself afresh! It is like cool water to the thirsty man, balm to the wounded spirit, healing to the soul. I bow, and weep, and worship.

He is with us in the battles, in the trials, in the defeats, in the daily humdrum tasks; with us in our weaknesses and when we fail; with us when souls are swept into the Kingdom; with us when we shout the victory. He is with us to guide us, to chastise us, to encourage us, to teach and instruct us. What a Friend, what a Companion! He is my present Saviour and my wonderful Lord. 'The LORD is with you.'

The programme of God

'The LORD your God is with you *wherever you go*.' It is interesting to note that these simple words were spoken once before to a very reticent, excuse-making Moses in Exodus 3:12, when he was called to face both Israel and Pharaoh. The same God gives the same assurance in similarly threatening circumstances to Joshua. It is a mighty word of encouragement.

It might be some far-off tribe, or it might be the cement jungles of the modern cities to which he sends us. It might be to do some menial task or it might be to take the leadership of some work which he has brought into being. It might be to the pulpit, the evangelistic platform or the mission field that he calls you. It might be in just one or many of the different tasks of gospel propagation in the modern world that your skills are needed. Remember: 'The LORD your God is with you wherever you go.'

With this great word we can encourage ourselves in the Lord. My enemies may be strong, but he is with me; even my friends may seem doubtful, but he is with me.

This is a wonderfully comforting word. It is also a convicting word, for if he is with me all the time, he sees all that I do and observes to what extent

I put my heart into the task. I walk before the omniscient One. I am therefore not only encouraged by his heart-warming presence, but I am also challenged because I am seen and known by him before whom no sin can stand. My life must be scrupulously clean for it is under divine scrutiny, and it is for me to walk in purity before the Lord in his perfect will.

Only as I am 'kept by the power of God' and as I 'keep myself pure' can I be assured of his presence with me, for he will not identify himself with sin. I must keep close to him through the cleansing blood, the indwelling Spirit and the enthroned Christ.

We then come to:

The plea from God

'Be strong and of good courage; do not be afraid, nor be dismayed.' Three times, in verses 6, 7 and 9, God commands Joshua to be strong. This clearly indicates that Joshua was not presumptuously over-confident and assertive. On the contrary, when the call came, his heart failed him. Far better that way, for then we are not relying on our abilities, thinking that we are sufficient for the job; rather we rely on God's omnipotence. He alone is able.

God said, 'Be strong', for Joshua, no doubt, felt weak; God said, 'Do not be afraid', for Joshua was fearful; God said, 'Do not be dismayed', for Joshua might consider quitting the job altogether. When God appointed him to responsibility he assured him of his presence and gave him such stirring commands that he could not refuse. God was with him.

MOTIVATED BY MOSES (DEUTERONOMY 31:6–8)

God had said to Moses, 'I will certainly be with you' (Exodus 3:12). When Moses was rejected by Israel and when he questioned God's plan in Exodus 4–5, God came to him (ch. 6) and assured him of his covenant, his self-revelation and his determination to have his promises fulfilled. He said, 'I will bring you into the land which I swore to give to Abraham, Isaac, and Jacob; and I will give it to you as a heritage: I am the LORD' (Exodus 6:8).

That God had been with Moses was certain. True, he had failed conspicuously on a few occasions, but God had given him strength to bear the burdens of the nation and to see the whole project through almost to completion. What an amazing accomplishment: an ongoing saga for forty years! God had certainly been with him.

Now, with all that experience behind him, Moses turns to Joshua and encourages him to trust this faithful God. He says: 'Be strong and of good courage, do not fear nor be afraid of them; for the LORD your God, he is the One who goes with you. He will not leave you nor forsake you' (v. 6). This he does in the presence of all the people (v. 7). It was at a public ceremony when the leadership was conferred upon Joshua that God gave Moses the very words for the new leader, words which God would give to Joshua directly a little later (Joshua 1:9).

When the leadership has confidence in up-and-coming new leaders they can pass on the baton with joy. Moses did just that. Joshua was God's choice, and God encouraged him through the retiring leader to govern effectively, for God was with him.

MOTIVATED BY THE PEOPLE (JOSHUA 1:16–18)

Notice:

Their petition for courage

'Only be strong and of good courage' (v. 18). Moses had said these words to Joshua in front of the people, and now they, in wholehearted agreement, echo them. Joshua must be hearing them by now! Moses told him, God told him and now the people tell him: 'Be strong.' He is being encouraged by everyone. How good of God to speak again and again until the message sinks in and is indelibly written on the heart: 'Be strong, for I am with you. Do not fear, do not be dismayed nor discouraged. I am the Almighty God who brought you out of Egypt. Now go forward, and trust me.' The people were with him!

Their promise to co-operate and obey

'All that you command us we will do, and wherever you send us we will go' (v. 16).

Joshua must have gained enormous inspiration and been filled with courage when the people declared their allegiance to him in this manner. How he must have thanked God! He would be able to work with a willing people.

Notice, though:

Their plea for commitment

'Only the LORD your God be with you, as he was with Moses' (v. 17). They wanted one thing and that was that Joshua would walk with God as Moses had done. They would then have confidence in him and would follow him anywhere. They had recognized that God was with Moses and now this was the one condition which they placed before their new leader. They laid it down for their obedience and co-operation: 'Joshua, you must be a man of God; then we will follow you!'

People will forgive you if you are not the best organizer or administrator in the world, if your sermons aren't as polished as they would like them to be or if you do not relate to young people or children as they had hoped; but they will not forgive you if you are not a man or a woman of God. This above all else is the qualification for the service of God. We must know God.

Moses talked with God. The people knew that and they had seen the holy light on his face. 'Joshua, you too must be familiar with the courts of heaven. You too must be able to enter into the presence of God on our behalf and come from the presence of God with a message from his heart to ours. You too must carry with you the awareness of the eternal.' They wanted to see God in the one who delivered his message.

People don't just want words. Today, there are many words: clever words, good words, even biblical and theological words, but people need words from God. We can have a great deal of good theology that carries no life because the man who is delivering it treats the Bible as an academic book to be analysed and taught, rather than God's word to be spoken to his heart and then through him to the congregation. He may be a good evangelical brother, but does he know the secret of the inner chamber? Does God speak to him? Has he a word from God? This he will only find if he learns to wait on God. This is the secret of holy unction, of the sacred anointing. How sad that there are so few burdened, unctioned preachers with a burning message straight from God's heart! May this cry from the people of God back in Joshua's day echo in our own hearts today. They will follow us if we minister with the touch of God upon us.

Note

1 **Alan Redpath,** *Victorious Christian Living* (London: Pickering & Inglis, 1956), p.30.

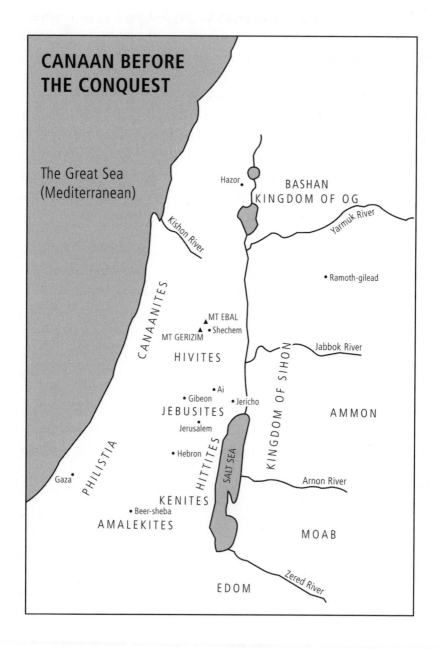

CANAAN BEFORE THE CONQUEST

The Great Sea
(Mediterranean)

Hazor

BASHAN
KINGDOM OF OG

Kishon River

Yarmuk River

• Ramoth-gilead

CANAANITES

▲ MT EBAL
▲ • Shechem
MT GERIZIM

HIVITES

Jabbok River

KINGDOM OF SIHON

• Ai
• Gibeon
• Jericho

JEBUSITES

AMMON

Jerusalem

SALT SEA

• Hebron

HITTITES

Gaza •

PHILISTIA

Arnon River

KENITES

• Beer-sheba

AMALEKITES

MOAB

EDOM

Zered River

The great commission (1:1–18)

Without a doubt, Joshua was being prepared for the day when he would be called upon to lead the nation of Israel. He had been spoken to by Moses and by the people, and now he was to be commissioned and charged by the Lord himself.

The exhortation

Joshua and those whom he led were to be governed wholly by the written Word. No one before Joshua had been required to regulate his or her life in accordance with the teachings of a book, but here was this Book of the Law with undeniable and unquestioned supremacy. From this time on the book was to govern the lives of all those who trusted in God. This was an historic introduction to the importance of the written Word: 'This Book of the Law shall not depart from your mouth, but you shall meditate in it day and night, that you may observe to do according to all that is written in it. For then you will make your way prosperous, and then you will have good success' (v. 8).

Four things are mentioned in this text as essential issues for those who are in leadership: the centrality and knowledge of the Bible, meditation on the Bible, obedience to the Bible—to which God adds his great assurances of prosperity and success—and the unity of the people of God (vv. 12–18).

KNOWLEDGE OF THE BIBLE

This was probably not a new idea to Joshua, for he had undoubtedly realized the importance of the law from Moses during the years of his association with him. If Moses had spent much of the preceding thirty-eight years working on these written documents, Joshua must have been a witness to that labour and must have come to value that law.

There is no escape! Life for those who belong to the Lord, and especially for those who are in a leadership position, should be lived out of the Word of God. We read in verse 8 that we must know it, that we must speak it, that we must think it and that we must obey it. We must therefore live in it. The best possible way to prepare for God's service is to study and get to know God's Word.

MEDITATION ON THE BIBLE

Meditation on the Word of God is not optional but obligatory. Joshua was commanded to meditate. This is one of the most important means of growth in grace. We too must meditate if we would progress in true spiritual and vital holiness.

It is not sufficient merely to read the Bible; the Bible must be studied and its teachings absorbed. 'You shall meditate in it day and night.' Biblical meditation will transform your life. Its continuing practice will give an ever-increasing knowledge of God. Biblical meditation is a divinely appointed way of coming closer to God. We will not grow without continual manifestations of God and meditation is one of the means of receiving such insights. Through meditation on the Word of God, the Spirit of God interprets the Word and we are strengthened by his indwelling sweetness.

Biblical meditation is the practice of pondering, considering and reflecting on verses of Scripture in total dependence on the Holy Spirit to give revelation of truth and meaning, and, by obedient response to that Word, having it imparted to the inner being. The impartation of such truth brings life and light. Meditation is inwardly receiving truth. It is feeding on Christ, the living Word. It is the devotional practice of pondering the words of Scripture with a receptive heart, allowing the Holy Spirit to take the written Word and apply it as the living Word to the inner being. The result is the impartation of divine truth.

As we meditate upon God's Word, there comes a fresh understanding which heals and cleanses our minds, which feeds and satisfies our souls and which quickens and strengthens our spirits. As the ideas and words of men swirl around us, we will know that we have found 'a place of quiet rest' where we can say with all humility, 'God spoke to me today.' This is how we get to know God. It is an open secret.

Meditation is the digestive faculty of the soul. It is like a cow chewing its cud. All day long a cow gathers the grass and stores it in the large storage stomach. Then evening falls and the cow lies down to chew its cud—it ruminates. Lumps of grass are brought up from the storage stomach and are chewed and swallowed again, being absorbed and digested in the other stomachs. There has been reception, deglutition, regurgitation, insalivation, mastication, ingestion, digestion and absorption! That is rumination! The black cow eats green grass and produces white milk and yellow butter. The grass has been absorbed into her system, has become part of her life and results in ongoing fruitfulness. People eat and drink and are strengthened by what that cow has absorbed and given away. Every growing Christian is a ruminating being!

Jeremiah wrote, 'Your words were found, and I ate them, and your word was to me the joy and rejoicing of my heart' (Jeremiah 15:16). The Word of God must become part of us. We must digest it and absorb it as we ponder its truths and meditate upon its teachings. Remember that the Lord Jesus was steeped in Scripture and was able to quote from it three times when tempted by the devil. He defeated the devil by saying, 'It is written …' He also said, 'The words that I speak to you are spirit, and they are life' (John 6:63). It is the word that he speaks to the heart, when we take time to meditate upon it and wait upon him, that brings life and light, and gives protection and power.

To know God is to love him, and it is from that intense and burning love that all service flows. Ezekiel records that he was told: 'Son of man ... eat this scroll, and go, speak to the house of Israel' (Ezekiel 3:1). His occupation with the Word inspired his service. He ate and then spoke. Biblical meditation increases our knowledge of and love for God. The Word of God and the love of God will then flow through us as life from God to others.

When you meditate constantly, God says, 'you will make your way prosperous, and then you will have good success' (v. 8). Biblical meditation increases the knowledge of biblical truth, arms against the assaults of the enemy, gives the understanding of God's mind on various issues, brings vibrant growth in grace, and leads to able and safe leadership. Meditation is everything.

This is the forgotten art in Western Christianity, and because it is not practised as it should be, we are correspondingly weak and powerless. Meditation is life-transforming. Learn to meditate on his Word.

OBEDIENCE TO THE BIBLE

'Observe to do according to all that is written in it' (v. 8, also v. 7). Not only did Joshua have to meditate upon the Word, he also had to obey it. He was not called upon to make new laws but to keep the ones already given. No one is above the law of God, and although Joshua was a man of authority, he was commanded not to turn from it 'to the right hand or to the left' (v. 7). He needed to be completely submissive to the legislation of his predecessor.

He was not to be regulated by his own inclinations, nor lean on his own understanding, nor be guided by expediency, nor seek to please folk by compromise; rather he was to obey what God said, and to obey *all* that God said. He was not to pick and choose the portions which he preferred to obey and disregard those which did not seem palatable, but rather place himself under the Word of God, seeing it as a single instructive unit.

Full obedience may involve numerous difficulties; it may make many enemies; it may face disapproval in the light of accepted norms. It could be very costly, so God encouraged Joshua, and, in turn, us, that he might fully obey his Word.

Will they think you strange when you obey God in your daily walk? What kind of price will you have to pay? It will require courage to swim against the tide. It calls for courage to ignore the sneers of those around you, but God assures you that, by obeying him, you will have good success.

There are other assurances as well. God says that he is 'giving to them' this land (v. 2). It is a gift and an inheritance which they will 'divide' (v. 6). The land is theirs! They did not work for it nor earn it, but they must possess it; it is a free gift from his gracious hand. In the spiritual realm we cannot work for all that we inherit in Christ. It comes to us from God as a free gift. It is for us to possess and occupy.

'Every place that the sole of your foot will tread upon I have given you' (v. 3). They would have to claim their inheritance and would need to do a lot of walking! The land is vast. There is always more land to be possessed. There is no room for complacency, but every reason for alacrity as we go forward to grasp our inheritance in Christ.

'No man shall be able to stand before you' (v. 5). No man—not a rebel from your own side nor an enemy from the other side. Comparing this with Deuteronomy 7:24 we see that, although God is addressing Joshua here, he is making this promise to the whole nation. If that was true for the Israelites of that day, it is surely true for us in the spiritual realm today. Are we claiming it? Are we being defeated by those people or things which stand before us? God promises us victory over them all. Let us rise up and believe God for that victory.

'As I was with Moses, so I will be with you' (v. 5). God's resources will never be exhausted. God's word, 'I will not leave you nor forsake you' (v. 5), made Joshua ready for any assignment. Even in our weakness, he will not fail us.

Chapter 6

THE UNITY OF THE PEOPLE OF GOD (VV. 12–18)

Joshua first instructs the nine and a half tribes going to the west of Jordan, and then addresses the two and a half tribes staying on the east of Jordan. The tribes who claim their possession to the east of Jordan must accompany those who are to cross the Jordan and fight the battles alongside them before returning to their own inheritance to the east of Jordan. There must be unity in Israel.

In the exhortation which he gives to the two and a half tribes, Reuben, Gad and half the tribe of Manasseh, Joshua affirms that which Moses had already laid down. The arrangements already in place were confirmed. They were to cross with the others until the land was subdued.

Notice how Joshua addressed the two and a half tribes. He did not beg them for their co-operation, nor did he argue that it would be good if they were to come. He pressed upon them the word of God! God had said that they must cross the river, and that they are bound to do. The servant of God honours God by applying the requirements of his Word. His own opinions count for little; it is the Word of God which must be upheld and obeyed.

It is interesting to note the concern for 'all Israel' throughout the book (see chs. 3–4; 7–8; 10:29ff.; 22:12,16; 23:2; 24:1). The unity of Israel throughout the book of Joshua forms a healthy contrast to the increasing fragmentation of Israel in the book of Judges.

Unity among God's people is no idle luxury: it is a necessity. Ruptures in the church have torn families and communities apart and have caused endless pain. People seem to be intent on devouring one other. What a sad breach in fellowship, what a disgraceful exposure and laughing-stock to the scornful world!

True believers need to be united in spirit and love through the death and resurrection of Jesus Christ, the indwelling Holy Spirit and the basic doctrinal essentials of the faith, even though they may be enrolled in different regiments of the Lord's army.

The commission

'Arise, go over this Jordan, you and all this people, to the land which I am giving to them' (1:2). We see here *compulsion* ('arise, go'), *direction* ('over this Jordan') and *possession* ('to the land which I am giving to them').

THE COMPULSION

God told Joshua to 'arise' and 'go'. The Canaanites were a numerous and powerful foe and those whom Joshua commanded a most unpromising people, but a man assured of the call of God is invincible. God will see us through and we shall see his promises to us coming true before our very eyes.

Jesus said 'Go' to his disciples, and that word has resounded around the globe. It moves the heart and fires the soul. The commission comes from heaven. The Christ who left heaven's glory and spent himself so utterly is in my heart urging me to go as he himself went. His presence within me responds to his mighty word to me—'Go!' I am caught up in the eternal thrust of God. I cannot escape it, for I am part of it; the word lives to me and the word lives in me—'Go!'

Jeremiah said, 'His word was in my heart like a burning fire shut up in my bones; I was weary of holding it back, and I could not' (Jeremiah 20:9). Amos said, 'A lion has roared! Who will not fear? The Lord GOD has spoken! Who can but prophesy?' (Amos 3:8). Paul echoes this spirit when he claims, 'The love of Christ compels us' (2 Corinthians 5:14), and again, 'Necessity is laid upon me; yes, woe is me if I do not preach the gospel!' (1 Corinthians 9:16). The call of God sends men and women to their neighbours and to the ends of the earth. God enables men to do impossible things because they are thrust into action by the Holy Spirit.

If God is laying his hand upon you, don't resist the call; he will guide you into his perfect will. What a privilege to be called of God; undeserved in grace and unparalleled in glory. Jesus said 'Pray the Lord of the harvest to send out labourers into his harvest' (Matthew 9:38). Perhaps you are the one whom the Lord is sending.

Chapter 6

God calls his children to his work and then sends them out into his service. Most people do not know where they will be working at the outset. He leads them as they follow him.

Joshua was now directed firmly and specifically—'over this Jordan'. How on earth was that to take place? Within the Jordan valley is the river's floodplain, which is up to one and a half kilometres (about one mile) wide. The floodplain was packed with tangled bush and jungle growth. Both the river and the jungle posed problems! In spring the Jordan's rushing waters (3:15) filled the floodplain, so they faced a raging torrent, between them and Jericho.

Isn't it amazing that Joshua did not baulk at the prospect? If God says it, then over this Jordan we will go, even with the river in full flood; wading through the waters, through the tangled growth, with our women, children, cattle and sheep. Some prospect! It was the river of death. Faith in a miracle-working God was now an absolute necessity.

Many of Joshua's 600,000 fighting men (Numbers 11:21) had died in the wilderness, but many more had been born and now took their place. With probably a few hundred thousand of an army he was about to enter a land consisting of an array of city-states. The heads of the city-states were called kings and all were generally independent of one another. 'Archaeologists have discovered that the typical city-state had a wall about 50 feet high and 50 feet wide.'[1] We read that Joshua defeated thirty-one kings in all (12:24)—some accomplishment!

The standard method of warfare was known as siege warfare; those within the city would do everything possible to prevent the walls being breached. Attackers would use battering rams and other devices to breach the walls. Sieges could often last two or three years, so, when the ten spies advised retreat, they were simply looking at things from a human standpoint and their conclusion was logical and correct. In no way could this group of slaves overcome the heavily fortified cities of Canaan. Israel had no engines of war and no strategy. The task was daunting—overwhelming! Just how was the victory to be won? Joshua and Caleb, however, looked beyond the human to God.

In the conquest of the land God firstly caused the walls of Jericho to fall down. Then the people of Ai left their city to rout the Israelite army—and Ai was taken. The kings formed confederacies to fight Joshua on the plain and they left their fortified cities so Joshua was able to defeat several at one time. With divine intervention the process took about seven years, and instead of the possible sixty to a hundred years, which siege warfare would have demanded, God gave them the victory suddenly, gloriously.

When we sense God calling us into his service, we also may be conscious of numerous difficulties in the way. There may be unavoidable circumstances which block our path. Sometimes family situations can be trying. There may be lack of finance, underlying fears of what friends and family would say, fears regarding marriage, fears of failure. These could all be dangerous deviations along the way. Yet nothing is too hard for our wonderful God! He can sweep these impossibilities away in a moment and can free us to follow his leading.

THE POSSESSION

'The LORD your God himself crosses over before you; he will destroy these nations from before you, and you shall dispossess them. Joshua himself crosses over before you, just as the LORD has said' (Deuteronomy 31:3); 'Every place that the sole of your foot will tread upon I have given you, as I said to Moses' (Joshua 1:3).

Here we see:

The vindication of his promise—'as I said'

This God is unchangeable. He has an unflinching purpose. If he has promised, he will make it good. He will never let us down. Hundreds of years had passed but the promise had not faded. What he had said to

Abraham would take place. He was now bringing them to the place which he had promised them.

The revelation of his purpose—'I have given you'

It was written: 'Then he brought us out from there, that he might bring us in, to give us the land of which he swore to our fathers' (Deuteronomy 6:23). God had overcome the difficulties and had set them firmly on the pathway to the Promised Land. Now they were here and the prospect of those promises being realized was an imminent reality. They were on the threshold of the coming settled occupation.

The demonstration of his power

The extent of the land is recorded in verse 4. The borders are indicated and the territory is briefly described. 'No man shall be able to stand before you' (v. 5). God is going to do battle for them: 'I will not leave you nor forsake you.' The task is beyond their abilities, but God will be with them.

When it seems that it is all impossible, God comes to our aid, assuring us of his presence, his purpose and his power. He will see us through the most impossible problems and bring us to that of which he has spoken to us. He will not break his word. He will fulfil his purposes despite the fact that we seem to be so weak and the task so impossible. He is the Lord God Almighty.

The action

'Prepare provisions for yourselves, for within three days you will cross over this Jordan, to go in to possess the land which the LORD your God is giving you to possess' (v. 11). He did not say, 'you may cross' or 'you shall attempt to cross', but 'you will cross'. This is the language of faith! Prepare, pass over and possess; those were the instructions.

God first commanded Joshua, then 'Joshua commanded the officers of the people', then the officers commanded the people. Notice that he did not call a conference of all the heads of the tribes to seek their advice, or to discuss the massive problems and difficulties. He acted when he knew what God wanted and he commanded the officers. There is a time for discussion, but there is also a time for decisive action when we are finally sure of the will of God.

The officers were to 'pass through the camp' and instruct the people. The whole nation was being mobilized for action. The verb used here (translated 'pass through') is the same as that used in verse 2 in 'go over this Jordan' and in verse 11 in 'you will cross over this Jordan'. It is a verb of action and indicates the atmosphere of activity and expectancy of these first chapters. The officers and the people were caught up in this great movement. The march was on!

In contrast to their hasty flight from Egypt, they now had time to make sufficient preparations. As Christians our spiritual food must be well-prepared lest we faint by the way. We must be 'nourished in the words of faith and of the good doctrine' (1 Timothy 4:6). We must take time to gather vital spiritual supplies for the battles ahead.

They were given three days to prepare. Three days—a picture of the resurrection. In three days the new nation was to be born in the new land. The crossing, when it came, almost took the appearance of a ceremonial act of worship and spoke in type of death beneath the waters—had they been there—and of the birth or resurrection of a nation on the other side of Jordan.

The only way for them to conquer the enemies on the west of Jordan was to pass through the river, a picture of death. The only way for us to conquer the world, the flesh and the devil is to pass through these waters of death and live in the power and strength of the resurrected Lord. God tells us to 'Reckon yourselves to be dead indeed to sin' (Romans 6:11). This is a matter of faith and as we identify with Christ in his death so we can also identify by faith with him in his resurrection and move on to victory ground, conquering the foes before us. We must lay hold of the fact that 'our old man' is 'crucified with him' (Romans 6:6), so that we can be 'raised with [him]' (Colossians 3:1) and live in his victory. This is brought about by the exercise of faith in what he did at the cross when he destroyed the power of sin and laid waste the forces of evil. Death is basic to the experience of the overcoming life in God. The doorway to victory in our lives is death to self-will, and then we 'walk in newness of life' (Romans 6:4). The cross is the heart of our emancipation, for as we die with Christ, so we also live with him.

It is not by increased devotions, vows and renewed consecration, nor by days of fasting and prayer, nor by any other thing that we shall enter the land of blessedness. It is by trusting that in our death with Christ we die to the evil which has overpowered us so often, has ruined our beautiful relationship with Jesus, has spoiled our testimony and has caused us private grief and confused sorrow. It is by identification with him in his death that we are released to life.

Then Canaan is ours! It is the purchased possession bought by Christ's precious blood. It is ours to possess now by faith, by laying hold on the promises of God. Notice that Joshua says, 'Possess the land which the LORD your God *is giving* you to possess' (v. 11). This land had been given to Abraham long ago but to these Israelites it was a present-tense gift. They had to claim it and possess it.

The promises of God have been made, and many have claimed them and entered into their inheritance in Christ in the past; but to every generation comes the necessity for personal trust in those promises. I have to claim my inheritance and possess my possessions, and so do you. We must all have personal dealings with God by faith and live in that which God so liberally gives us in Christ.

Powerful foes will attempt to prevent the people enjoying their heritage, so strenuous efforts will be required. Only as they implicitly obey the commands given to Joshua will they be victorious. We too must meet the divine requirements to obtain the divine inheritance. Obedience is a key word in the book of Joshua, and it is a key word for us as Christian men and women.

Note

1 **Thomas R. Rodgers,** *The Panorama of the Old Testament* (Newburgh, IN: Impact Press, 1988), p. 73.

Rahab (2:1–24)

The people were poised to cross the river and Joshua made the final preparations. Forty years had passed since they had left Egypt. Had Joshua been in this particular region at all when he was sent as a spy, he would have forgotten most of it by now. He now despatched two spies across the river to examine the area and assess the mood of the people. Joshua did not assume that God placed any premium on ignorance. In sending just two spies, did he remember that nearly forty years ago only two spies had returned with a good report? Note that these men were completely *anonymous*. God often works through ordinary people of no particular renown or ability. These were exciting and exhilarating moments.

The spies entered Jericho and found the house of the harlot Rahab. This would be the most inconspicuous of entries, for few would question their presence in the house of a harlot. We read that they 'lodged there' (2:1); they did not go there for immoral purposes. Rahab might have been running a lodging house or a kind of bed-and-breakfast business, and the spies were quick to take note and to find shelter there. Here they would be least likely to be asked embarrassing questions. But they were seen, and the search for them was on. The enemy is watching *our* every move, too, and will oppose all efforts to forward God's cause.

Rahab hid them in her house, misdirected the men who were looking for them, extracted a promise of mercy from the spies, helped them to escape and promised her co-operation. By all these things it is evident that she had turned from her heathendom and embraced the God of Israel. She is mentioned as one of the heroes in the great chapter on faith: 'By faith the harlot Rahab did not perish with those who did not believe, when she had received the spies with peace' (Hebrews 11:31). What a fascinating person she is! But who exactly was she?

She was a Gentile

Rahab was an '[alien] from the commonwealth of Israel and [a] stranger from the covenants of promise, having no hope and without God in the world' (Ephesians 2:12). She had none of the advantages of those who were being guided by the moral principles which God had laid down in his Word. She had been brought up in the immoral and evil customs which characterized the heathendom of that day. God is sovereign in his choice of those whom he uses. He used the heathen king Cyrus to send the Jews back from their captivity. Here he uses someone who is quite outside of the people of God to accomplish his purpose.

She was a woman

In some cultures, women are held in very low esteem and have very few rights. In fact, in some countries women are even regarded as objects to be owned. In many parts of the world they live as second-class citizens. Here God chooses to use a woman. Women may have different roles, but they too can be called of God and exercise valuable ministries.

She was a Canaanite

In fact, she was an Amorite. It would appear that the Amorites were particularly evil, for in Genesis 15:16, the Lord names them as those whose cup of iniquity is not yet full. But now, full it had become, and they, together with all the other nations who were practising evil, were about to receive the punishment that was their due. The Amorites were a corrupt, vile people, even sacrificing children in their depraved religious practices. They were ripe for judgement. Rahab's god could well have been the Egyptian god Ra, for that was the beginning of her name.

She was a prostitute

Rahab, here called a harlot, was a woman who had formerly been of ill fame, the reproach of which stuck to her name, though of late she had probably repented and reformed. Simon the leper (Matthew 26:6), though cleansed from his leprosy, wore the reproach of it in his name as long as he lived; so with Rahab the harlot. The stigma of sin may abide for years.

Rahab could well have already ceased from her evil practice, for she hid the spies 'with the stalks of flax, which she had laid in order on the roof' (2:6). Flax was laboriously gathered by industrious women and laid out on the tops of houses to dry for use in spinning and weaving. She herself had laid it all in order on the roof and there was sufficient there for men to be able to hide beneath it. This seems to indicate that Rahab had turned from her immoral lifestyle and was now earning a decent living in society. Although she may have been living, as it were, on the edge of society, it would seem more likely, because of her questing spirit and living faith, that she was being usefully employed in the spinning and weaving industry.

Whether she had been, or was still, engaged in sin, she now had a seeking heart and an enquiring mind. She was emerging from pagan darkness into a faith in the God about whom she was hearing. She heard the tales of what God had done for the Israelites and she knew that her people were terrified. She may have heard some of these tales in the market place but she could also have had firsthand accounts from the men who frequented her home. It was a good talking shop. The spies chose their cover well. They would hear much in the house of Rahab.

Perhaps God had sent them there for the specific purpose of rescuing this child of God from the inevitable judgement which was soon to fall, for, although Joshua had no need to know about Jericho's internal structure, she had need of being delivered. In a similar way, Lot was rescued from wicked Sodom. God often rescues his own from impossible circumstances.

She showed strong family concern

She very commendably showed strong and tender concern for her relatives (2:12–13), pleading for them to be spared with her in her house, but there is no mention of her own children. Father, mother, brothers and sisters are all mentioned, but no children. Perhaps she did have children, but, if so, they were the responsibility of someone else at this point and were not with her.

She heard of the people of God

Stories had been circulating about these special people who belonged to the God of heaven and earth. So should it always be with God's children. Unbelievers should realize that in their midst are people who are different and wholesome, who are in touch with a God of whom they know very little, if anything at all. These people are a separated and holy people, who pray and derive their way of life from a Book, the Word of God. They live kind, upright, honest, moral, exemplary lives, and these lives make an impact. They are the people of God. Are our lives causing people to stop and think? When they watch us, will they have cause to admit that God is with us and that we are walking with him?

She heard of the power of God

She heard that the Lord had dried up the Red Sea forty years ago. She heard how the Israelites had utterly destroyed Sihon and Og, the two kings east of Jordan (v. 10), 'and as soon as we heard these things, our hearts melted; neither did there remain any more courage in anyone because of you' (v. 11). The news of these remarkable events brought awe and fear to the people of the land. 'Faith comes by hearing' (Romans 10:17). She heard enough about God to be able to place her trust in him. She honestly confessed her utter helplessness. Fear of the sudden judgement filled the hearts of those around her. '[Some] save with fear, pulling them out of the fire' (Jude 23). Here is one who was groping her way from heathen darkness as she was finding faith in the Creator God.

She believed

'I *know* that the LORD has given you the land' (v. 9, emphasis added); 'The LORD your God, he is God in heaven above and on earth beneath' (v. 11).

She had heard about this wonderful God and this knowledge was the basis of her faith. 'I know'—this is the conviction and assurance of her faith. There was no 'if', or 'perhaps' or 'I hope' at all. It was a certainty. She holds to the utter supremacy of *Yahweh*. She assumes that he is the only God functioning in heaven and on earth. Here is a pagan Canaanite coming to faith; from prostitute to proselyte, from darkness to light. The commitment was total and irrevocable. From this point on she was to be counted among the people of God, even if she were the only one in Jericho. When she trusted in the God of Israel, she stood alone. If it had become known that she was trusting in the God of the enemy, there could have been serious consequences. Sometimes it's a lonely business to believe in God when everyone in the family, at the workplace, school or university seems to mock the things of God. It calls for commitment and perseverance as we continue to believe in the face of indifference, apathy or violent opposition.

Notice that she says, '*I* know', not '*we* know'. Many heard, and the hearts of many melted with fear, but her hearing and knowledge led her to faith. Her faith was personal and genuine. Many who hear the good news today turn away from God.

She worked

James says that Rahab was justified by works: 'Likewise, was not Rahab the harlot also justified by works when she received the messengers and sent them out another way?' (James 2:25). Not that the works saved her, but the works were the outward evidence of a vibrant faith. We are justified by faith alone, but the faith which justifies is inevitably accompanied by works, which are the evidence of that faith. James says further, 'I will show you my faith by my works' and 'faith without works is dead' (James 2:18,20). She had now come to faith, and that was obvious to any observer who knew of her activities. She hid the men with the flax on the roof of her house (v. 6). She later helped them to escape: 'She let them down by a rope through the window, for her house was on the city wall' (v.15). The inward reality was breaking out in practical activity. Do our works, our lives, show that we have saving faith? Can others, observing us, recognize immediately that we serve the holy God of heaven and earth?

She deceived

After she had received the spies, the king of Jericho sent to her and demanded to see the men. She had hidden them in her house, but she replied that, although the men had been with her, they had now left the city. If she had told the truth, God would doubtless have delivered the men some other way. How could Rahab be justified by God and proclaimed a hero of faith when what she said was so obviously wrong? She had deceived and lied. This is an ethical dilemma. God calls his children to be people of integrity. Rahab's lie cannot be condoned or disregarded, but it should be remembered that she was a pagan woman whose heart and mind were just beginning to be opened to spiritual things. Perhaps her lie was a sin of weakness in one whose conscience was just being awakened out of heathen darkness.

She had courage

She knew that the true God was with the Israelites and that they were moving forward victoriously. She was, however, part of her own people and city. If she hid and guided the two spies, thus helping the invading forces, she would most certainly be seen as a traitor and be done to death. If she included her parents and brothers and sisters in her survival package, they would all have to be told, and this would increase the possibility of her betrayal being inadvertently leaked by one of the family members. She put her life on the line. She risked her own life and the life of her family for the sake of the spies because she now repudiated her past and embraced the new life with the people of God. She did not have much time to think, but she did have the courage to make a tough decision.

Not only do we need to be available to God, but there also comes a time when we must be willing to take action. Are we willing to pledge ourselves to him without knowing all the answers and without seeing the end of the road? Rahab committed herself! She took the leap of faith and launched herself on the God of heaven and earth, the God whom she had now come to know and trust.

She obeyed

The condition on which her house would be spared was that she would bind a scarlet cord in the window through which she let them down. The invading forces would not spare anyone outside the house with the scarlet cord, but all those within would be safe. She said, 'According to your words, so be it.' She sent them away and *immediately* 'she bound the scarlet cord in the window' (vv. 18–21). When you know what God wants, it is always good to do it immediately. Delayed obedience and partial obedience are so often disobedience.

Furthermore, she tied the cord which they had specified. She did not substitute a blue or white line of cord. Her obedience was exact. God requires exact obedience, however small the issue.

While the Israelites at Kadesh Barnea did not enter the land because of unbelief and disobedience, Rahab was saved because of faith and obedience. The scarlet cord was the sign of the covenant which she had made with them, and her immediate and precise obedience gave evidence of that covenant being established. Her obedience arose out of her faith. She believed in Israel's God, and so hid the men and helped them in their enterprise, co-operating freely with them in it.

She tied the scarlet cord

There is a tradition in the church that the scarlet cord represents the blood of Jesus and that this scarlet thread goes all through Scripture, from Abel's sacrifice to Calvary.

There is a remarkable parallel between the cord that marked her house and the blood of the lambs spread on the doorposts of Jewish homes in Egypt when the angel of death passed over the land. In Egypt, all died who did not have the blood on the lintels of their doors, and here in Jericho, all died who were not in the house which had the red cord in the window. They were saved by that red cord.

If we understand her story, we can identify with Rahab. We, like her, were originally not part of God's family at all, but were part of a corrupt, degenerate society. Rahab then heard of God's mighty deeds among his children, and in the same way we heard of God's work of salvation. God then brought messengers to us, just as he did to Rahab, who told us more of the realities of God and of his people. He drew us out after him and we stood before the choice of life or death. By his grace he enabled us to trust him and to launch our all on the One who called us. We believed, as Rahab believed. We were called to repudiate the old society and life to which we had belonged and identify ourselves with the family of God. As a sign of that, the blood of Christ was the token in our lives and homes. That red cord was hung in our window with the assurance given us that we now belong to the people of God. We are saved from the awful judgement and now have a new family.

What if you have given no heed to that which you have heard of God and of the people of God? What if, when messengers were sent to you, you ignored their exhortation and warning? What if, in your self-confidence, you said, 'The walls are strong, the city will stand'? Remember that there is a day of certain judgement coming. Your strong walls will tumble down and you will be unable to withstand the wrath of Almighty God. You will be called to account, your sin will be exposed and then the dreadful judgement will fall and you will not escape.

Why shouldn't you be like Rahab? All she heard were distant stories of God and his deeds. You have the light of the gospel shining all around you in this dispensation of grace. The sacrifice of Jesus atones for our sins. The Holy Spirit applies Christ's work to our hearts and brings us into a saving relationship with God. Why should you live any longer under the condemnation of God? Turn from your sinful past, trust this Saviour to be your own personal Saviour, and take your place with the people of God.

She triumphed

'Joshua spared Rahab the harlot … So she dwells in Israel to this day' (6:25). She was able to take her place among the people of God and live happily with them.

She married a man called Salmon, settled down and had a family in Israel. We have this wonderful record of her family in Matthew: 'Salmon begot Boaz by Rahab, Boaz begot Obed by Ruth, Obed begot Jesse, and Jesse begot David the king' (1:5–6). Her son Boaz was King David's great-grandfather and in direct line to Joseph, who had the privilege of welcoming the Son of God into his home.

'By faith … Rahab did not perish' (Hebrews 11:31).

She is an example of faith

As an example of faith, Rahab is outstanding. In this chapter we see many facets of her faith.

- The risk of faith: 'She had brought them up to the roof and hidden them with the stalks of flax' (v. 6).
- The certainty of faith: 'I *know* that the LORD has given you the land' (v. 9).
- The understanding of faith: 'I know that the LORD has given you the land' (v. 9).
- The courage of faith: '… the terror of you has fallen on us' (v. 9).
- The hearing of faith: 'For we have heard how the LORD dried up the water of the Red Sea for you' (v. 10).
- The confession of faith: 'For the LORD your God, he is God in heaven above and on earth beneath' (v. 11).
- The prayer of faith: 'Now therefore, I beg you … spare my father, my

mother, my brothers, my sisters, and all that they have, and deliver our lives from death' (vv. 12–13).

- The obedience of faith: She was told to 'bind this line of scarlet cord in the window ... And she bound the scarlet cord in the window' (vv. 18–21).
- The patience of faith: She had to remain silent about the whole matter until it took place. 'And if you tell this business of ours, then we will be free from [this] oath' (v. 20).
- The victory of faith: The spies said to Joshua, 'Truly the LORD has delivered all the land into our hands' (v. 24).

Rahab's life brings many precious aspects of spiritual life to us. May these lessons be well learned and bring us, through faith, to a living, saving relationship with the God who saved her and who is ready to do the same for us now.

The crossing (3:1–4:24)

'T hen he brought us out from there, that he might bring us in, to give us the land of which he swore to our fathers' (Deuteronomy 6:23). This was the objective. Now the Israelites stood before the flooded river Jordan with the immediate prospect of entering the land.

God would cause the river to dry up for several reasons:

- It would enable an immediate and easy entry into the land.
- It would facilitate instant military occupation.
- It would reveal his power to a new generation. The God who could dry up the Red Sea was the same God who would dry up the Jordan. The new generation would witness the power of God over nature.
- Joshua's position would be confirmed, because he predicted the event and it came to pass. He would be seen obviously to be God's chosen successor to Moses.
- The awesome spectacle of a nation crossing the river would cause the inhabitants of Canaan to be devastated psychologically. They would have felt secure because the flooded river formed a natural barrier to any hostile force, but once the hordes poured over the dry riverbed, 'their heart melted; and there was no spirit in them any longer' (5:1).

The preparation

Joshua had told the people that they were to prepare for the crossing, for in three days they would cross the river (1:11). They were to prepare physically, so they made provisions for the journey. They were to prepare psychologically; these three days would be used profitably in preparing mind and heart. There would be time to rest, pray, encourage one another. They were to prepare spiritually: 'Sanctify yourselves, for tomorrow the

LORD will do wonders among you' (3:5). This principle still holds. There must be a time of spiritual preparation before any great event. Jesus spent the night in prayer before he chose his twelve disciples, and if he needed to pray, how much more do we!

God was about to drive out from before them seven nations (3:10). By this act of God, they would 'know that the living God is among you'. This would be an experiential knowing (Hebrew: *yada*). They would know, not only with their understanding, but also with their heart, that 'God is with us!'

God told them that they had 'not passed this way before' (3:4). These are words of consolation, direction and expectation. Fear would not diminish the danger, and the God whom they served had never let them down; so they could be comforted. He was directing them, so they were to hear his word and prepare their hearts to follow him. As they did so he would be to them all that they needed. Here in his presence, they would be prepared for all that lay in the unseen future.

Joshua had hundreds of thousands of fighting men, so the number gathered on the banks of the Jordan could not have been fewer than two million. (Forty thousand armed men prepared for war from the tribes of Reuben, Gad and half the tribe of Manasseh crossed over with all the others, 4:13.) The crowds must have stretched for miles along the river! The wonder is that they gathered there without murmuring or questioning. We don't read of any dissent. But to attempt the crossing would mean certain death, and they knew it. How could mothers and babies, pregnant women and children, sheep and cattle cross the swollen, one-and-a-half-kilometre-wide river (for 'the Jordan overflows all its banks during the whole time of harvest', 3:15)? Yet they gathered in expectancy and faith. The crossing would need to be accomplished in the daylight hours of a single day. They did not know how it would be accomplished, but they knew that their God would not leave them stranded on the east side of the river. This was a massive act of faith in the face of impossible circumstances.

Not only were the great difficulties of crossing the river woefully apparent, but what of the dangers of the foes on the other side of the river? If they ever got across, there would be no going back, and they would immediately have to face the wrath of the nations with all their weaponry and experience of war.

Yet no word of complaint is recorded as they gathered with the expectation of faith. They had a great God and he would see them through! God was in control of the people, the events, the circumstances and even the enemies. They would trust in him! Oh, may God give us such uncomplaining, expectant and trusting hearts, so that we, like them, would believe that he is big enough for any eventuality or impossibility! We are not sufficient—but he is, and we can trust him.

The ark

No longer did the pillar of fire lead them. They were now led by the ark, which represented the presence of God. The ark was a box made of shittim or acacia wood and covered with gold; it was 1.5 cubits broad (0.7 metre), 1.5 cubits high and 2.5 cubits long (1.1 metres). It is known as the 'ark', the 'ark of the covenant' or the 'ark of Testimony'. It was to be carried by the priests to the middle of the river and held there until all the Israelites had passed over the Jordan. The people had to maintain a respectful distance of 2000 cubits (about 900 metres) from the ark. It could not be treated casually. This would also prevent crowding around the ark, keeping it in full view of all the people all the time. The ark dominated the crossing:

- the ark to be seen (3:3);
- the ark at the brink of the Jordan (3:6);
- the ark to be borne by priests (3:8);
- the ark into the Jordan (3:11);
- the ark in the Jordan—waters cut off (3:13);
- the ark in the Jordan, ahead of the people (3:14);
- the ark borne by priests on dry ground in the Jordan (3:17);

- the ark in the Jordan—waters cut off (4:7);
- the ark in the Jordan—twelve stones set up to mark the feet of the priests (4:9);
- the ark carried across after the people (4:11);
- the ark comes out of the Jordan (4:16);
- the ark out of the Jordan—waters return (4:18).

Every development and event is linked to the ark. This is not Joshua's crossing or war; God was in control and he was leading them into a conflict that would destroy the Canaanites and all their vile iniquity.

The ark supremely represented Jesus Christ. It was made of wood, signifying his humanity, and completely covered with gold, speaking of his deity, all beautifully blended in one unit. Here we have typified the deity and humanity of Jesus Christ: 'God … manifested in the flesh' (1 Timothy 3:16). God as man—one Christ, one glorious Person—is presented to us here. The wood and the gold were moulded together. This is a revelation of the incarnation. God deigned to identify with man by actually uniting with him in this intensely intricate, personal and mysterious way. God and man blended together in Jesus Christ. 'God was in Christ' (2 Corinthians 5:19).

The ark was covered by the mercy seat, which was a slab of pure gold. It formed the lid of the ark and was placed in the Most Holy Place in the tabernacle in the wilderness. Only once a year did the high priest enter the Most Holy Place to make atonement for the sins of the people. When he did so, on the Day of Atonement, he sprinkled blood on the gold slab. The blood of the earthly sacrifice trickled onto the gold, which represented deity. Again there is this strange and marvellous union. Here is Christ's sacrifice: the shedding of his precious blood as an offering for our sins. Here is Calvary. This is where God meets man! 'There I will meet with you' (Exodus 25:17–22).

Here then, the incarnation and crucifixion are typified in one item of furniture—the ark. These two great events are inextricably linked together. Bethlehem and Calvary are inseparable. It is here, pointing to Christ, that God meets man.

In the ark were three things:

- The golden pot containing manna—a picture of Christ's life and provision for his people.
- The two tables of the Covenant with the Ten Commandments, which Christ alone kept perfectly.
- Aaron's rod that budded, a picture of Christ's resurrection.

Everything in and about the ark spoke of the future Christ. Just as the ark led the way into the waters, so Christ precedes his church. 'But each one in his own order: Christ the firstfruits, afterward those who are Christ's at his coming' (1 Corinthians 15:23). 'When he brings out his own sheep, he goes before them; and the sheep follow him' (John 10:4). It is our duty to 'follow the Lamb wherever he goes' (Revelation 14:4)—even into Jordan. 'Their king will pass before them, with the LORD at their head' (Micah 2:13). He is 'the author and finisher of our faith' (Hebrews 12:2). He is the Alpha and Omega of our salvation. He was the first to go into Jordan and the last to come out of it. He was there until everyone had crossed. His death was effective for all the redeemed. He is our salvation.

The entry

The day for the crossing dawned—what a day!

Soon the waters were to be cut off at a town 'very far away at Adam'(3:16). It has been thought that the town of Adam was twenty-four to thirty-two kilometres (sixteen to twenty miles) upstream. There is no agreement as to its precise location. We are not told whether a 'natural disaster' blocked the river or not—but if it were some natural obstruction like an avalanche, it certainly was a miracle that it occurred just at that precise moment. The riverbanks and riverbed drained and the Israelites were able to walk across quickly (4:10) 'on dry ground' (3:17).

Moses was dead, representing the law, for the law could not bring anyone into the spiritual land of promise which the prophets saw afar off but did not inherit. Joshua, representing the Lord Jesus, was God's appointed saviour to take them into the land of promise, which, spiritually speaking, was purchased for us by the Lord Jesus: the land of the fullness of the blessing of the gospel of Christ.

This land was only attained by faith in God, who told them to enter the waters of death.

What, then, is the spiritual teaching of this crossing of the river? Much emphasis is laid upon it in the New Testament, for example: 'I have been crucified with Christ; it is no longer I who live, but Christ lives in me' (Galatians 2:20) and 'You died with Christ', 'you were raised with Christ' (Colossians 2:20; 3:1). We see this particularly in Romans 6:1–11, where the following words occur: 'buried with him … into death'; 'united together in the likeness of his death … we also shall be in the likeness of his resurrection'; 'If we died with Christ, we believe that we shall also live with him'; 'Reckon yourselves to be dead indeed to sin, but alive to God in Christ Jesus'. The teaching of these passages is that in Christ's death the believer died, and in his resurrection the believer was raised to live a new life.

Early in the morning the millions gathered near the waters' edge. At last a little group emerged from the crowds. It was the group of priests slowly descending to the water, bearing on their shoulders the sacred ark with the golden lid and the cherubim. The procession moved ever nearer to the waters of death. What madness! The waters showed no sign of receding but seemed to wait maliciously for the priests' feet to enter so that they could execute their evil design and plunge the whole nation into a dreadful death by drowning. But in the hearts of the priests and of the leaders was faith in the God to whom they were committed and from whom they had received the orders to walk towards the waters. They would trust for a miracle! They marched forward in silent and determined obedience and faith.

At last, as the people gazed intently, the feet of the priests dipped into the waters, brown with mud, foaming in their hurried rush. Then the miracle took place; the waters began to divide and shrink away. As the priests pursued them they fled before them as if panic-stricken. 'What ails you, O sea, that you fled? O Jordan, that you turned back?' (Psalm 114:5).

Here is a picture of Jesus leading the way, dying, and death fleeing before him. He dipped his feet in death, and dying, abolished death. It fled before him as Jordan fled before the priests who carried the ark. He was made to 'taste death for everyone' (Hebrews 2:9), and in doing so he has 'abolished death and brought life and immortality to light' (2 Timothy 1:10). The ark advanced on the shoulders of the priests and as it advanced, so the waters fled. With what authority did Jesus enter the realms of death!

At the end of that dreadful day in Jerusalem, he cried out triumphantly, 'It is finished!' He died, but in his death he vanquished death. Now, for those who believe in him and who follow him as the people followed the ark, 'Death is swallowed up in victory. O Death, where is your sting? O Hades, where is your victory?' (1 Corinthians 15:54–55). Death is swallowed up in life.

What an amazed and triumphal procession crossed the Jordan that day! They should have died in the swellings of Jordan, but they lived! That which had prevented them from inheriting God's promises was removed when they believed God. It was the ark that led the way! Jesus has opened up a new and living way for us. We now have access to all of God's riches through his death and precious blood. For the Israelites, now the promises were theirs, the land was theirs and God's riches and full blessing were theirs. Passing through Jordan was but a transition from one form of existence—that of wandering aimlessly in the desert—to another which was far more useful, purposeful and satisfying: that of life in a settled community where agriculture, animal husbandry and, consequently, riches would result. Abundant life replaced an insecure and anxious one. It is the same today: those who are identified with him in his death live with him in his vibrant and overflowing life. They enter by faith into the river of death, identifying with the ark, with the One who has gone before, and pass through with him on to the other side.

We will never get into the land of promise if we stand unbelievingly on the brink. Are you on the brink? It may seem impossible that the Lord would ever be able to liberate us in the Spirit and set us free from the many things which may bind us as children of God. How would God ever be able to release you from the vile temper which erupts every now and again? How would God be able to deliver you from all the unclean thoughts which at times plague your mind? How would God be able to save you from the spirit of jealousy which defiles and cripples you? How could you be free from hypocrisy, from cover-up? And that grudge that you have been holding for years? No! It is impossible! The river is too wide. It cannot be crossed. God cannot deliver you. You are on the brink. You will just have to turn back and die in the carnal wilderness of wistful longings and weak living. Canaan may be for others, but you just don't seem to be able to meet the requirements and enjoy the blessings.

Multitudes of Christians reason just like that! They live lives which are deprived of victory because of their failure to believe that which God says he will do! They suffer with the 'wretched man' of Romans 7 who tries to do good but cannot, and who does not wish to do evil, but cannot stop himself from doing it. They may be regarded as exemplary Christians, but they know in their hearts the moments of defeat and sad failure. They wish that they could be different and are sometimes grieved by their inability to live as they wish they could. This shuts their mouths, for, because they do not experience victory, they feel that they have no right to talk about the wonderful salvation in Christ. The whole cause of Christ is prevented from making the advance that it should, simply because the believer is frustrated in his or her unsatisfactory Christian experience. They are standing on the brink. Are you standing with them there?

When the writer to the Hebrews reviewed these events he said that God had appointed a day for them to move into the promised land, and that day was 'today'. 'Let us … be diligent to enter that rest'—'today' (Hebrews 4:7–11). Now is God's time. The Holy Spirit says 'today' lest the hardening process begins and becomes habitual. Every delay is dangerous. Today, renounce selfish attitudes; today, reach out to that which God offers you in Christ. 'Today leave the wilderness forever, and enter by faith the Land of Promise.'[1]

Look at the ark! Look at it! It is there in the middle of the river of death. Come and identify yourself with it and walk with Jesus the path of death that leads to abundant life. It is a definite committal of self in all its devious forms. It is saying goodbye to the world, to our past life and everything in our present life which is less than the will of God. It is an identification with the cross of Calvary. All that which displeases him must be brought to the cross to die.

Oh, we will do anything but die! Our great show of consecration to the work of God can merely be a manifestation of self so that others can see how dedicated we are. We can make all sorts of sacrifices, giving and working, but these can all be revelations of self-centredness. The hidden sinful egocentricity baffles us in our search for his purity and power. It lurks in the innermost recesses of the soul.

We are always afraid that it will be discovered by some unexpected incident, and that we will be exposed before the discerning eyes of our fellow believers. But God forces it out into the open. To expose self-love without its mask is a mortifying experience. Oh, allow him to strip self-love of every adornment until it stands barren and exposed! Now see yourself as you really are. It's not a pretty sight!

How glibly we speak and sing of going to Calvary, but only one thing happens at Calvary—death! If the Red Sea crossing typifies God's judgement on sin, the Jordan crossing typifies his judgement on self.

Still standing on the brink? Is the death too painful, too demanding? You'll never get to the land with all its riches in Christ on the other side of the river, never inherit all the promises, never know the blessings and benefits, the fullness of his love and Spirit, if you keep standing on the brink. What does the cross mean to you? Let the Holy Spirit apply this question to your heart: Have you died with Christ?

Look, so many are crossing. Don't just stand there! Keep your eyes on the ark, on Jesus, on the cross. By faith identify yourself with the cross there in the middle of the river of death. Walk! Walk by faith! He is dying for you. Now, by faith, die with him. Not only is this substitution, it is also identification. Say by faith with Paul, 'I have been crucified with Christ; it is no longer I who live, but Christ lives in me' (Galatians 2:20). Believe it. 'For he who has died has been freed from sin. Now if we died with Christ, we believe that we shall also live with him' (Romans 6:7–8). Trust the One with whom you not only die, but also will emerge in the newness of resurrection life! You are with him in death and now you are with him in life. The land is before you—it is yours! Possess it! 'They could not enter in because of unbelief. Therefore, since a promise remains of entering his rest, let us fear lest any of you seem to have come short of it … There remains therefore a rest for the people of God' (Hebrews 3:19–4:1,9).

And in the river, build a memorial at the place where the feet of the priests were placed, right there where the ark had stood—a memorial to death, death with Christ. 'If One died for all, then all died' (2 Corinthians 5:14). That means me. In him I die, with all the others. Claim this great truth by faith. The ark is in the centre of the river, picturing Christ in his death. We die with him, and rise again with him, too.

And on the other side, build another memorial—a memorial to life, life with Christ. 'But God … even when we were dead in trespasses, made us alive together with Christ … and raised us up together, and made us sit together in the heavenly places in Christ Jesus' (Ephesians 2:4–6). We are on resurrection ground. We can avail ourselves of all our lofty privileges, girded with the power of the risen, living Jesus. The ark has emerged from the river. Death gives way to mighty resurrection life.

What aids to faith these memorials were! The people could look at them again and again and remember the wonderful deliverance God had wrought. Down the years parents would tell their children what these stones meant: Their great God had led them through. If he had done this for them, they could trust him for anything. He would not let them go until all his purposes were complete. What wonder, what worship and gratitude, did the sight of those stones inspire!

We must never forget God's mighty acts in grace. Build the memorial and remember. When they come in later years and ask, 'What are these stones?' (Joshua 4:21), you will be able to answer that those spiritual memorials were built when God performed the miracle in your life, and brought you into identification and conformity with his death to set you free to enjoy him and all the lavish gifts of his love. It was the moment when you entered into something very wonderful and found the great secret of losing your life and finding it in God, when God came to take full possession and control of your whole life, and filled it with his own. It was something to which you can look back with great joy and humble gratitude. You can now enjoy the full blessing of that which he has done, and, in him, find precious heavenly communion with the One who has brought it all to pass.

The exaltation of Joshua

'And the LORD said to Joshua, "This day I will begin to exalt you in the sight of all Israel"' (3:7). The exaltation of Christ as the God-Man dates from the moment he stepped into the hurrying waters of death and dried them up. 'The God of peace … brought up our Lord Jesus from the dead, that great Shepherd of the sheep, through the blood of the everlasting covenant' (Hebrews 13:20).

He sets the joy-bells ringing when he frees the soul to rest from all those inward strivings; when he breaks the bands of cancelled sin; when he brings us to his banqueting house and sets his banner of love over us. He is exalted in our hearts in a new and wonderful way. Why, he is Lord of all now! He is the Bridegroom of our hearts! He reveals himself in such precious ways that we kneel in worship and adoration. He ravishes our hearts! Ah, yes, it is all worth it! Praise his wonderful Name!

God showed the nation that, just as he had been with Moses, he was now with Joshua. It was the continuity of leadership which God had promised. The spirit which had been upon Moses was now upon Joshua—and they saw it! He was but Moses' servant before, but now he is exalted before the people by God's authority which rests upon him. In this leadership position, all he did was direct the people to look to the ark and to follow it! Look to Jesus! Look to Jesus! Follow him. He will lead you through to victory! That is all a leader must do—point the way to Jesus Christ!

Note

1 **F. B. Meyer,** *The Way into the Holiest* (London: Marshall, Morgan & Scott, 1950), p. 54.

Four significant events (5:1–15)

The kings' hearts 'melted' (v. 1). They had felt safe enough in their walled cities even though they were threatened by the approach of this rabble company on the east of Jordan, but now, that which they had heard in connection with the Red Sea had taken place right on their doorstep. The Jordan had miraculously parted and this nation was on their home ground. Who could fight against such a God? They quaked with fear; there was no more spirit in them and their hearts melted. What God had promised in Exodus 23:27 was taking place: 'I will send my fear before you, I will cause confusion among all the people to whom you come, and will make all your enemies turn their backs to you.'

Four significant things happen in this chapter:

- Circumcision is instituted.
- The Passover is celebrated.
- They eat the grain of the land and the manna ceases.
- The Commander of the Lord's army appears to Joshua.

Gilgal

They had reached the west bank and set up camp at Gilgal, which was to be the base of operations throughout the war. There the camp remained, with the women and children (9:6; 10:6). Gilgal was a very significant place for Israel. It was a place of *relief, renunciation, remembrance, restoration, resurrection* and *revelation*.

It was here that the 'reproach of Egypt' (v. 9) was rolled away, for Gilgal means 'rolling'. The reproach of Egypt was, firstly, that they were despised slaves in Egypt; secondly, that they were tainted with the idolatry of Egypt

(Exodus 32:1–6); and thirdly, the scoffing jeers of the Egyptians that, although God had taken them out of Egypt, he could not take them into Canaan (Exodus 14:3). After all those terrible years in Egypt, and after the long years in the wilderness, they stood at last as free men, on the land which God had promised to their father Abraham. They were in their own land and they were free! The reproach was rolled away! It was at this place that the Commander of the Lord's host appeared, and stated that this was holy ground.

What if the two and a half tribes settled east of Jordan? They were still part of the twelve tribes, for there were twelve stones. Even after the ten northern tribes had broken away from Judah after Solomon's death, they could be reminded that they were once united, as all twelve tribes had stood together on that spot—there were twelve stones.

Samuel was later to exercise his ministry among the three towns of Mizpah, Bethel and Gilgal (1 Samuel 7:16). It was from Gilgal that Elijah would begin his last epic journey with Elisha before he was taken up into heaven (2 Kings 2:1). Gilgal was a significant place in Israel's history.

Rebellion and restoration

'The people came up from the Jordan on the tenth day of the first month, and they camped in Gilgal' (4:19). This month was the first month of their year. This was instituted in Egypt, where they were commanded: 'On the tenth of this month every man shall take for himself a lamb' for the Passover (Exodus 12:1–5). God keeps memorials and anniversaries with meticulous precision. Forty years had elapsed and now, after they had wandered so far from him in disobedience, they were returning to his plan. But for their rebellion at Kadesh Barnea, the Israelites could possibly have been in Canaan forty years before. What stopped them? Unbelief and disobedience!

Sin keeps back the blessings of God, and the consequences of doing wrong lead us into weary wandering—perhaps years of weary wandering—away from the full purposes and blessing of God. They went the way of their choosing; they got what they wanted and many died in the wilderness as a consequence. Now, however, they were returning; and we too can return, whatever our sin has been and however far we have wandered from him. He brings us back to begin again, for there is mercy with the Lord. They were beginning again with God—and so may we.

CIRCUMCISION IS INSTITUTED (VV. 2–9)

'All the people born in the wilderness, on the way as they came out of Egypt, had not been circumcised' (v. 5). The mark of the covenant which God made with Abraham was circumcision. He said that he would give to Abraham 'all the land of Canaan' (Genesis 17:8), and the sign of this covenant was that 'every male child among you shall be circumcised' (v. 10). It was to be mass circumcision. They had broken the covenant relationship with their God in that they had refused to believe and obey him at Kadesh Barnea. But God was true to his covenant, and now he had restored them and brought them into the land which he had promised them in Genesis 17. Circumcision was to be re-instituted, for the covenant was being renewed. God was the covenant-keeping God. He was faithful to his promise.

There would be temptations in the land where so many pagan nations practised all their vile religious rites, so the people were being reminded that they belonged to a holy God. They would always know that they were his people because they bore the mark of the covenant.

This physical operation on the body was meant to be a symbol of a spiritual operation on the heart. 'Therefore circumcise the foreskin of your heart, and be stiff-necked no longer' (Deuteronomy 10:16). This is the 'circumcision made without hands, by putting off the body of the sins of the flesh, by the circumcision of Christ' (Colossians 2:11). 'Circumcision is that of the heart, in the Spirit, not in the letter' (Romans 2:29). 'Circumcise yourselves to the LORD, and take away the foreskins of your hearts'

(Jeremiah 4:4). Circumcision to them was the outward evidence of an inward reality. God had put up with their rebellion in the wilderness but now they were being restored and were to live according to his word. They had previously walked in disobedience to him in the wilderness, but now they were to cut away their stiff-necked rebellion.

Circumcision speaks of the crucifixion of the flesh. We are to put away the old man and his deeds—anger, wrath, malice, envy, pride and evil-speaking. Circumcision is putting off the body of the sins of the flesh. Without this there can be no victory in Canaan. This is absolutely necessary for all those who would live a life of victory in Jesus. This is Gilgal! We can never have victory, we can never take Jericho, until we have been circumcised, until God has taken away our self-reliance, and has brought us down to the dust of death.

Have you been hindered by carnality or worldliness in your testimony? Have you been missing the blessing of the Lord in your life? Perhaps you have refused his leading? You are arguing with God. In the process you have lost your joy. He has been ready to take the knife and go deep into your heart, but you fear the consequences. You still have your own plans and you want to see them through. Perhaps it's a friendship that needs to be broken; perhaps a habit from which you need to be freed; perhaps a position at work which you don't want to relinquish for the work of God. Ah, don't move away from Gilgal until God has completed his work. He is waiting for your surrender so that he can apply the knife to that which should not be there.

Previously we had the picture of dying with Christ in the Jordan and entering into a new land of victory and abundance. Here is another reminder. The truth is emphasized again: The old life of disobedience is now to be cut away and the people are to begin a new relationship with God.

THE PASSOVER IS CELEBRATED (VV. 10–11)

Israel's first Passover was observed in Egypt. The lamb was slain and the blood applied to the lintel and doorposts to enable them to escape judgement from the angel of death (Exodus 12).

Israel's second Passover was observed in the Wilderness of Sinai (Numbers 9:5).

Israel's third Passover is celebrated in the Promised Land (Joshua 5:10).

Immediately after the rite of circumcision was instituted, the Passover was celebrated! Circumcision was the necessary precondition for participation in the Passover festival (Exodus 12:48). After the knife had done its work there was the blessing. There must be a removal of sinful practices and carnal strivings; a cutting away of fleshly involvements; an identification with Christ in his great work of crucifixion; a yielding to him to do his will alone—then comes the blessing. In Israel the knife had done its work physically and now those who were wholly separated to the Lord were able to commune with him in a feast of remembrance, joy and hope. Gilgal is therefore the place of *restoration* and *rejoicing.*

Here on 'the plains of Jericho' (4:13), on the fourteenth day of the first month of the year, called Abib, later also called Nisan (4:19; Exodus 13:4; Nehemiah 2:1), they celebrated the Passover. The family gathered together for the sacred feast and reviewed the past with gratitude. They thought and talked of God's mercy to them and of the enormous fact that their redemption by blood in Egypt lay at the basis of their very existence.

How can we ever forget that it was because of Calvary that we are brought into God's favour? However much we may speak of sanctification and of the necessary death with Christ before we inherit all the riches of God, we must never forget that the basis of it all was justification by blood (Romans 5:9). However far we might have progressed in grace, we cannot but return to Calvary—where 'Christ, our Passover, was sacrificed for us' (1 Corinthians 5:7)—and bow in worship. We are saved by his blood. We look back with gratitude and adoration to the One who died for us. Paul says, 'Therefore let us keep the feast' (1 Corinthians 5:8). He does not say when and where we are to keep it. It is to be a perpetual feast of gratitude and joy as we daily feast on the Lamb of God. Jesus tells us that, as we eat his flesh and drink his blood, we abide and live in him (John 6:51–58). 'He who feeds on me will live because of me' (v. 57). May it ever be our experience to stand with our waist girded with the truth, always feeding on the Lamb of God, ready for whatever he wants us to do and wherever he wants us to go.

But let us also remember that, just as no uncircumcised person could partake of the feast, no one living in wilful sin can feed on the blessed Lamb of God. You will not be strengthened by his life if you are out of step with him. There must be a Gilgal before there can be a Passover.

THEY EAT THE GRAIN OF THE LAND AND THE MANNA CEASES (VV. 11–12)

Something dramatic happened: They ate the produce of the land! A whole generation of people had become dependent on the miraculous daily appearance of the manna that God had provided—and now there was grain! Their diet was changed. What a strange taste! The day after they had eaten the grain, the manna ceased, and its passing ended a forty-year miracle.

The grain could have been either from the previous year's harvest or from the present barley harvest.

The Passover reminded them of their deliverance from Egypt, and the manna reminded them of their desire to go back to Egypt; for when they lusted after the fleshpots of Egypt (Exodus 16:3), God gave them food from heaven which they picked up every day for forty years. Now it was all over and they would have to work to provide their own food. Their circumstances had changed and they had to adjust. They were no longer in the desert but in an agrarian environment, and they would have to be introduced to agricultural methods and eat the fruit of their labour. Change is difficult for most of us. It is often painful, but change is a fact of life, and God's resources help us to adjust to the inevitable changes that occur.

It was unleavened bread that they ate on that first day after the Passover. The Feast of Unleavened Bread began on the fifteenth day of the month, and lasted seven days (Leviticus 23:6). Here in the land they ate unleavened bread.

In all these events we have a brand new beginning. There is the circumcision, the Passover and the unleavened bread, with the manna now ceasing. These were momentous days which were never to be forgotten. They had entered a new period in their history. To eat the paschal lamb was the first step, but now they are introduced to the rich foods of the land of Canaan.

We must feed on the Lamb, but then also on the grain of the heavenly land, and derive benefit and blessing from his resurrection life. Not only do we die with him by passing through the river of death and by 'eating the Passover' to commemorate the event, but we also live in him in his resurrection life on the other side of the river. The food is rich! It includes bread and spiritual fruits that grow on resurrection soil. There will be milk and honey. There are stable and well-built homes. There is much to gain from the land of Canaan! It is far removed from that uncertain, nomadic existence in the arid, burning wilderness.

We remember that he died and we with him, but now he lives and we in him. 'In him we live and move and have our being' (Acts 17:28). We take his risen life, we meditate on his Word, we commune with him and live in the manifestation of his presence to our souls. He has given us abundant life as we move into this new, full relationship with him. Come over into Canaan-land, you who are in the harsh, barren, burning desert. Come, taste and see that the Lord is good, so very, very good!

Just remember that those who were unbelieving and disobedient perished in the wilderness. The new generation of Israelites entered into their inheritance by faith in God, but their parents and grandparents died in unbelief. Unbelief does not inherit promises. They died in disobedience. Don't perish with them there!

Gilgal, therefore, was a place of:

- *Memorials*, for the stones told the story of God's mighty power and great deliverance. They should have perished under the rushing waters, but they followed the ark into 'death' and now lived in the land of promise. The stones were a witness to it all.
- *Dedication and the renewal of the covenant*, for circumcision was instituted. They now had the physical mark of divine ownership and they would always know that they belonged to God. They were his forever.
- *Joy and Freedom*, for the reproach of Egypt was rolled away. God can roll away all the past with its shame, spiritual poverty and bondage. There is freedom from guilt, idolatry and from the fear of man. The reproach has gone.
- *Rest*, for it was 'the place where they lodged' (4:8). They had left the weary wandering and now had a place where they could remain and be at peace.
- *Sacrifice*, for here they celebrated the Passover with its offerings on the fourteenth day of Abib, the first month of the year. The lamb was selected, separated, sacrificed, shared and sustaining. So we feast upon the Lamb of God.
- *Remembrance*, for at the Passover they recounted all the mighty deeds of salvation. Salvation by blood meant separation from Egypt. They remembered that their loving heavenly Father protected them and provided for them on an untried way.
- *Change*, for they now ate food from the new land. Christ is the bread of life and we feed on him, living in the victory of his resurrected life. As we are identified with him in death and life, we too, with him, will conquer in and through his mighty power.
- *Dependence on God*, for the land, with all its impossibilities, still had to be conquered. They could not do this in their own strength, but only in the power of God. In him they now placed their trust. Let us trust the

One who leads us forward in victory.

THE COMMANDER OF THE LORD'S ARMY APPEARS TO JOSHUA (VV. 13–15)

Before Moses returned to Egypt to deliver the nation of Israel, God appeared to him in the burning bush and told him to remove his sandals from his feet, for the place where he was standing was holy ground. Before Joshua leads the nation into the Promised Land, he too has an encounter with the divine and is also told to take his sandals from his feet, 'for the place where you stand is holy'. Joshua was to have a reverent attitude of heart and mind. No man is ever the same after he has been brought face to face with God. What Joshua needed most was to hear from heaven, and God was there to meet him.

There is interruption

The burdens of leadership bore down upon Joshua as he walked alone and pondered the extraordinary events of the past days. It must have been a time of anxious suspense for the lonely chieftain. Perhaps he was meditating and praying. Perhaps he was taking a look at the city of Jericho and assessing its fortifications for the possibilities of its overthrow, for the incident took place 'by Jericho'. Suddenly, 'he lifted his eyes' and saw the Stranger. In the midst of difficult and pressing circumstances it is necessary, isn't it, to lift our eyes—maybe we too will see him.

The Warrior suddenly stood before Joshua with a drawn sword in his hand. He was in combat readiness. This was unexpected and dramatic. Poor Joshua, was he not burdened enough with the tensions of the past days? The last thing he needed was a life-and-death struggle with an unknown assailant, but now, right before him, stood a Man with a drawn sword. What was he to do? God sometimes interrupts us in our pondering and planning. He sees how we are trying to work things out in our own strength, and he interrupts us—sometimes quite dramatically—for he has a better plan.

There is an exclamation

Brave Joshua was *courageous* and walked up to the Man exclaiming, 'Are you for us or for our adversaries?' Joshua knew of only two armies. He knew of no middle ground of compromise and challenged the Stranger as to his position. He was not ruffled by the suddenness of his appearance nor daunted by his attitude of attack. He was also *concerned* for the people and their cause, and showed that there was to be no neutrality.

There is identification

This was a theophany, a pre-incarnation appearance of the Lord Jesus in the Old Testament. To Abraham he had come as a traveller, to Jacob as a wrestler, and now he comes to Joshua as the Supreme Commander.

When Cornelius fell at Peter's feet 'and worshipped him ... Peter lifted him up, saying, "Stand up; I myself am also a man"' (Acts 10:25–26). When the priests of Zeus wanted to sacrifice to Paul and Barnabas, the apostles cried out in protest, 'We also are men with the same nature as you' (Acts 14:15). When John fell at the angel's feet to worship him, the angel said, 'See that you do not do that! I am your fellow servant ... Worship God!' (Revelation 19:10). But when Joshua prostrated himself before this Man with the drawn sword, there was no prohibition to his humble worship. In fact, the awesomeness of the event was emphasized by the command to 'Take your sandal off your foot, for the place where you stand is holy.' This is none other than a visit by Jesus Christ to the earth prior to his incarnation.

There is a declaration

The heavenly Visitor states firmly, 'As Commander of the army of the LORD I have now come.'

Joshua had most certainly been wondering how he was to lead this motley group of desert wanderers to victory against the might of these fantastically fortified cities. Now the heavenly Warrior declared that he had not come merely to assist Israel's leader, but to control the whole operation. The responsibility would be completely lifted from Joshua's shoulders. He had not come to champion Joshua's cause; he had come to rout the enemy. He was, and is, to be recognized and consulted as Commander and in no other role. He is Lord. Our weak fighting efforts do not stand a chance against the devil's power and experience, but Jesus has come as Lord! Christ can perform his mighty works when we give him his rightful place.

The question should not be, 'Are you for us or for our adversaries?' but 'Are we wholly on your side?' We would align ourselves totally and completely with you, Lord Jesus, and all your plans for us. Lead us forward in your victory, our Lord and our Supreme Commander.

There is adoration

'And Joshua fell on his face to the earth and worshipped.' How essential that, before he stood fearlessly before the enemy, he fell prostrate at the feet of his wonderful Lord! He now had to deal with God himself. Oh, how utterly essential it is that those going into battle for the Lord first of all fall at his feet in adoration! Meeting God brings a light to the face, a spring to the step, joy to the heart, tenderness to the conscience, love to the soul and humility to life. It causes words to be full of his power and unction. It brings the presence of God into meetings. God is our exceeding joy! Our hearts break at the sight of his love and mercy. This prostration of spirit is all-important for the preacher and for anyone who wishes to live and work for the Lord. Do you know anything of this brokenness of spirit? Oh, what a precious trysting place it is when he reveals to us who he is!

There is submission

Joshua said, 'What does my Lord say to his servant?' Joshua had surrendered his command. His own strategy was insufficient and he handed over the reigns to the Commander-in-Chief. On this personal crisis the success of the whole campaign rested. The Lord was now in control. In public, Joshua was the strong leader and military general, but in private, he was the servant, hearing from God and obeying him. God directs the battle and leads the way.

However difficult the way ahead may be, let us not be fearful, for if we humbly and submissively enjoy the revelation of his presence, we have nothing to fear. We need not be preoccupied with our impregnable Jerichos, but we can rest in our omnipotent God.

The conquest of Jericho (6:1–27)

The conquest of Canaan was accomplished by three military campaigns—central, southern and northern. The central campaign, designed to divide and conquer, consisted of two major engagements: one at Jericho and the other at Ai.

The assessment of the problem and the strategy of war

Jericho was an ancient city. It was the bastion of strength for the land of Canaan because of its strategic location adjacent to the Jordan River. The conquest of Jericho was to be a symbolic victory. If Jericho could fall, then what other city could stand in their way?

They had to conquer Jericho! This powerful fortress barred Israel's progress. Its capture was vital if they were to conquer any other part of the country. Also, with Gilgal being only a few miles away, Jericho had to be conquered if the camp at Gilgal was to be left in peace. If Jericho remained unconquered and Joshua led his men away to fight in other areas, it would leave the camp at Gilgal vulnerable to a devastating attack by Jericho's 'mighty men of valour' (v. 2). In addition, it would enhance the reputation of Israel among all the inhabitants of the land if they knew that Jericho had been conquered by the invading forces. Finally, the capture of Jericho would also be a tremendous psychological boost to Israel in the early stages of the war.

THE INSTRUCTIONS FOR VICTORY

All the Israelites had to do was to walk around the city! First would come the armed men; then seven white-robed priests, blowing probably

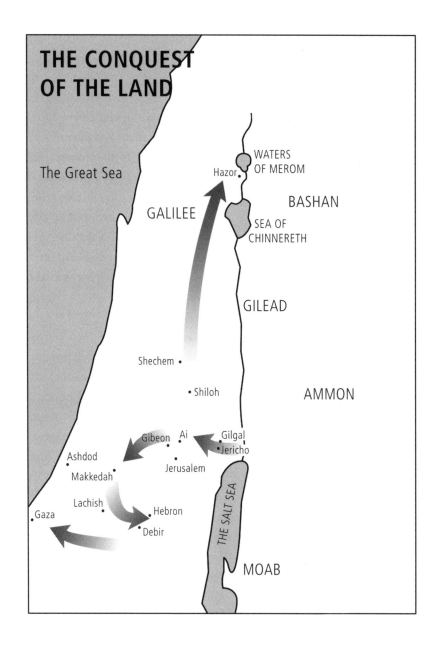

THE CONQUEST
OF THE LAND

The Great Sea

WATERS
OF MEROM

Hazor

BASHAN

GALILEE

SEA OF
CHINNERETH

GILEAD

Shechem

Shiloh

AMMON

Gibeon   Ai   Gilgal
                Jericho

Ashdod

Makkedah   Jerusalem

Lachish   THE SALT SEA

Gaza   Hebron

Debir

MOAB

discordant music upon their ram's-horn trumpets; then the ark, the symbol and token of God's presence; and then the rest following. The ark was in the centre. They had to encircle Jericho once a day for six days and seven times on the seventh day. On the seventh trip on the seventh day, the priests were to 'make a long blast with the ram's horn' (v. 5), which would be the signal for the Israelite soldiers to shout. The wall of the city would fall down flat and they would advance straight before them and take it.

The ark was especially mentioned and meticulously positioned. Joshua 'had the ark of the LORD circle the city' (v. 11). That was the issue. The important thing was not only that they compassed the city, but that the ark compassed the city, and that they were with it on its journey. The ark, of course, represented the presence of God and the person of the Lord Jesus. This symbolizes the victory we have through the presence of God, and, in particular, through the person of the Lord Jesus himself. It was God's battle and he was in the midst of his people.

THE UNREPENTANT PEOPLE OF JERICHO WERE WARNED

'Jericho was securely shut up because of the children of Israel; none went out, and none came in' (v. 1). It was shut up by the obstinacy of its inhabitants. None went out as deserters, or to offer terms of peace, and none came in, lest they be taken for spies or enemies. They acted 'defiantly against the Almighty' (Job 15:25). Their hearts were hardened to their own destruction. Jericho had to fall! So shall it be with all evil and unholy practices. God's judgement awaits them.

The priests of the holy God of Israel announced that God was declaring war on the wicked practices in Jericho. They blew the trumpets, sounding an alarm, so that the sinners might fear. The priests were God's heralds denouncing iniquity. We too are God's priests and need to speak clearly of things which are contrary to the holiness of God, proclaiming a warning to sinners and judgement on sin. By our very righteous living we speak volumes to those who are outside Christ.

Day after day the silent army of Israel passed before the Jerichoites. Only the constant shrill blast of the trumpets pierced the air. It is the will of God that men should be warned, for he has 'no pleasure in the death of the wicked' (Ezekiel 33:11). He warns that 'The soul who sins shall die' (Ezekiel 18:4,20). 'Cast away from you all the transgressions ... For why should you die?' (Ezekiel 18:31).

Those in Jericho could have recognized the danger which threatened them by the armed men who led the procession. They could have realized the certainty of an Israelite victory which was set before them by the trumpet-blowing priests. These men were making no pretence of celebrating a victory that had not yet occurred. They should have feared when they saw the ark of the covenant itself. They knew of the Red Sea crossing, the victories in the wilderness, and the parting of the Jordan River. This covenant-keeping God was before them for evaluation. They did wrong by keeping their gates closed to him. The patience of a long-suffering God had been displayed. The seventh day brought intensified warnings, but they did not heed those warnings and judgement fell.

The Jerichos that stand in our way

'There is the Jericho of sin. There is the Jericho of indifference. There is the Jericho of materialism. There is the Jericho of paganism. Worse than that there is the Jericho within the church of disloyal Christians, of unconsecrated lives, of people who have become so used to sinners going to hell that they don't care.'[1] These Jerichos seem to be altogether unconquerable. We have tried to batter them down with our preaching, teaching, efforts, counselling and with our earnestness and prayers, but we end up in despair after years of struggle. Our Jerichos laugh at our weak attempts to dislodge them. They are there in full strength. Where is our God?

Our Jerichos need the power of God to shift them. God is able to cleanse us and rid us of those seemingly unconquerable Jerichos which block our spiritual development. Don't go on any longer with that Jericho barring the way. Don't be taken up with the powerful walls; look at your all-powerful God. Believe that he can rid you of the Jericho and trust him to do it! Remember that ten spies saw their God through the mighty giants in the land, and as a consequence saw themselves as grasshoppers. Two spies saw the giants through their mighty God, and as a consequence became conquerors! They surged forward in faith to possess the land. Follow the two! Do not despair, but trust.

THE PEOPLE OF GOD WERE ENCOURAGED

While the daily march spelt judgement on the Jerichoites, the blowing of the trumpets was a great encouragement to the Israelites, for the blast of a trumpet was, in Jewish feasts, the solemn proclamation of the presence of God. It was their priests who were announcing that their God was coming in power to give them victory.

Further, it was the priests who blew the trumpets in triumph as they carried the ark, and this signified that the Lord was with his people in the day of battle. The ark was there. Their God was with them. This was an enormous encouragement to them and a boost to their morale. The God who had brought them through the Red Sea, and through Jordan, was here with them as they confidently marched into the land which he had long ago promised to them and was now in these very moments giving to them.

The inexplicable test

Christians who come through the wilderness into the land of full salvation discover to their amazement that, immediately, Jericho confronts them. To many this is incomprehensible. They expected to be overflowing with joy and glory, having trusted God when they walked through the Jordan, leaving the wilderness forever behind; but they are now confronted with a massive problem and face an enormous test. Satan is alive and active and wants to rob us of our new-found joy and victory. Suddenly, after the act of faith in crossing Jordan, we are in a major battle.

After Jesus was baptized he was led by the Spirit into the wilderness to be tempted by the devil. The blessing at the river was followed by a severe trial. After the blessing, the battle; after the fullness, the fight. Faith must be tested. In 1 Peter 5:7 we are told to cast all our care upon Jesus. There is the act of faith; yet immediately afterwards, in verse 8, we read: 'Be sober, be vigilant; because your adversary the devil walks about like a roaring lion, seeking whom he may devour.' Cast your all on God, trust him fully—and now remember, you have an enemy! 'Resist him, steadfast in the faith' (v. 9). 'Resist the devil and he will flee from you' (James 4:7).

THE INSPIRING WORDS

The Lord (the same person as 'the Commander of the LORD's army', 5:15) said, 'I have given Jericho into your hand' (v. 2). What a promise! For the leader, wondering how victory is to be attained, there is suddenly a word from God. What a change it makes to have a word from God! How important it is not to dwell on all the difficulties, but to focus on the promises. That did not mean that Joshua could sit down and do nothing. Promises do not eliminate responsibility; rather, they spur us on to action and further obedience.

The test of faith

How would these unskilled desert nomads use battering rams and throw up scaling ladders against the mighty walls that towered menacingly and victoriously over them? There seemed to be no answer to the problem of the walls of Jericho.

Down the years, the people of God have discovered that what is utterly impossible to man is no problem whatsoever to God. When countries are closed to missionary work, somehow God opens the doors; when finances are low and hope fades from the horizon, somehow God provides. God is a God of miracles. With him it is as easy to speak a word to our hearts as actually to make the impossible happen. Let us trust him in the darkness until the light shines.

In spite of the impossibility of the task, Israel's spirits were high. But God said, 'You will do nothing in this battle. The battle is mine. I will show you that, when you are confronted with an impossible task, I will see you through and the victory will be mine. All you need to do is trust me.'

Faith, mighty faith, the promise sees,
And looks to God alone,
Laughs at impossibilities,
And cries, 'It shall be done.'[2]

The prerequisite of faith

'By faith the walls of Jericho fell down after they were encircled for seven days' (Hebrews 11:30). It is the New Testament that tells us that the walls fell by faith.

'Faith comes by hearing, and hearing by the word of God' (Romans 10:17). You must have the word if you are going to have faith, for it is the foundation of faith. The Israelites certainly had the word, for God gave the command to Joshua and he relayed it to his people. They acted upon God's instructions and marched obediently, if with incomprehension, around the city. If you believe and trust, then you can obey. 'Without faith it is impossible to please him' (Hebrews 11:6). 'Faith is the substance of things hoped for, the evidence of things not seen' (Hebrews 11:1).

Faith is founded on the word of God. When the nobleman came to Jesus and implored him to come and heal his son who was at the point of death, 'Jesus said to him, "Go your way; your son lives." So the man believed the word that Jesus spoke to him, and he went his way' (John 4:50). He soon discovered that the boy had been healed at the very moment when Jesus spoke the word. He had a word from the Master! 'He believed the word'; that was sufficient! Jesus had spoken and it was sufficient.

God's word to our hearts is all-important. Upon that word we can place our trust. With that word we can go to the ends of the earth. With that word we can establish missionary societies, build churches, conference centres and Bible colleges. The word of God changes our lives and brings us into his ongoing purposes.

So shall my word be that goes forth from my mouth;
It shall not return to me void,
But it shall accomplish what I please,
And it shall prosper in the thing for which I sent it (Isaiah 55:11).

The obedience of faith

As had happened at the Jordan, the amazing thing was that the people believed Joshua and obeyed. They had not heard the Lord issue his orders, for these he had given to Joshua alone. They only had Joshua's word for it that these instructions were from God. They had to believe that God had spoken to Joshua and that he had told him to tell the people to act in this strange way. Some test! To them it must have seemed to be ridiculous beyond words! No army in the history of human conflict had ever received such preposterous commands. But they trusted throughout the long week of incomprehensible marches. They believed and obeyed.

Divine commandments may sometimes seem strange to fleshly wisdom. How absurd for Naaman to be told to bathe in the river Jordan for his leprosy to be cleansed; how unreasonable it must have seemed to the disciples for Christ to attempt to feed the five thousand with five small loaves and two fishes; why should the servants fill the jars with water when it was wine that was required at the marriage in Galilee? But these Israelites had crossed Jordan! The God who could perform such a miracle could give them the city of Jericho, too. So even if it were beyond their understanding, they would obey him! It will be to our good to obey Omniscience!

The grim silence of it all as they tramped, tramped, tramped must have been very impressive. The shrill discordant blasts from the priests' trumpets made eerie listening. To the Jerichoites it must have been awesome at first, but as the days wore on they probably felt more secure in their strongly fortified city.

The discipline of faith

Joshua had told the people, 'You shall not shout or make any noise with your voice, nor shall a word proceed out of your mouth, until the day I say to you, "Shout!" Then you shall shout' (v. 10).

Jeers and scorn probably poured down the walls of Jericho as the silent army wound its way around the city. They were probably out of range of the arrows from the wall and thus out of hearing of actual taunts, although they would have been conscious of the tumult.

Yet they had to preserve strict silence. If they had been allowed to talk on the journey they would probably have aired their doubts and fears. Why, there was not even a crack in these powerful walls! 'What are we supposed to be doing? Is this all just a sick joke?' They would have talked themselves out of faith, for unbelief is unbelievably contagious. But they had to shut up! This is probably the most remarkable example of united obedience recorded in the Scriptures.

The passion of faith

Joshua and the priests 'rose early in the morning' (vv. 12,15). This is the spirit in which to approach all our tasks and responsibilities. They were inspired to obey! It is much easier to lead people who are inspired by the Spirit's inward persuasion than those who need to be asked to obey instructions. It needs far more than instructions to get things done. In Nehemiah's day 'the people had a mind to work' (Neh. 4:6) and the wall was built in record time. 'Whatever your hand finds to do, do it with your might' (Eccles. 9:10). It is the spirit in man which drives him to great deeds;

and the Lord prompted the Israelites to respond and act. Their great God would carry them through to victory.

The perseverance of faith

Once around the city every day for six days and seven times on the seventh day—thirteen times in all, and all in silence! At first there must have been great excitement, but the days were passing, passing, passing. Be patient! Don't take the work out of God's hands. Don't try to wriggle out and do it in your own strength when you have committed yourself to his purpose. Travel on! Today is the fifth day; tomorrow is the sixth day; the next day is the seventh. Hold steady. 'The LORD ... will suddenly come to his temple' (Malachi 3:1).

Promised deliverances must be expected in God's time. After the victory on Mount Carmel, Elijah prayed for rain and sent his servant seven times before the news came that a cloud the size of a man's hand had appeared (1 Kings 18:42–44). 'It is good that one should hope and wait quietly for the salvation of the LORD' (Lamentations 3:26). 'My soul, wait silently for God alone, for my expectation is from him' (Psalm 62:5). 'For you have need of endurance, so that after you have done the will of God, you may receive the promise' (Hebrews 10:36). 'Therefore the LORD will wait, that he may be gracious to you' (Isaiah 30:18).

Jesus said that 'men always ought to pray and not lose heart' (Luke 18:1). How often we have fainted and lost heart when victory was in sight! We become discouraged when our Jericho does not fall after the first time round. Discouragement is one of Satan's most successful tools. How we need the grace of patience, 'for in due season we shall reap if we do not lose heart' (Galatians 6:9). Paul prayed for the Colossians that they might be 'strengthened with all might, according to his glorious power, for all patience' (Colossians 1:11). It would seem that patience is one of the highest graces that a Christian can have. We would do well to learn this great quality by faith and be enriched by it at all times.

The perils of faith

When judgement falls on the city of sin, everything must be put to the sword. Nothing in this wicked city must be spared. All its treasures of gold, silver and valuable goods must be preserved and consecrated to the Lord. No one must take these goods for him- or herself, for they are the Lord's. There is to be no plunder, with loot carried away in triumph. The people are forbidden to seize the spoils of war. It is God's battle and it is his victory.

There is no triumphal self-exaltation in the victory of faith. We cannot take the glory, for it is God's alone. 'Not unto us, O LORD, not unto us, but to your name give glory' (Psalm 115:1). When the wonderful new church is built, when the missionary society is at last well organized and effective, when the administration is well run, when you have preached a great sermon and many have sought the Lord, when finances roll in and the work is well established—don't take the glory. It is his alone! We are but unprofitable servants, doing what is ours to do. Faith takes no credit for the victory, but rather humbles us to the dust.

There is always the possibility that we should touch the glory of God. He says, 'My glory I will not give to another' (Isaiah 42:8). We bow low before him and worship him, for he has revealed his power and accomplished his purpose; we just happened to have the great privilege of being there when he did it. We cannot put out our hand to snatch the gold and silver and boast of our great deeds. How sad that some have touched the glory and thought of themselves more highly than they ought to think. Pride enters in and the dangers of falling from spiritual heights to the depths are frighteningly real. Keep humble; keep holy in the midst of victory. Pass the test!

The assurance of faith

They had continued so bravely and had persevered so obediently, for they were certain that the Lord whom they served would come to their aid. God had said to Joshua, 'See! I have given Jericho into your hand' (v. 2). This inspired them to continue to march in silence day after day, and not to flee in fear.

When their obedience and patience had been fully tested, the command was at last given: 'Shout, for the LORD has given you the city!' (v. 16). They shouted when the powerful walls still stood intact! It was therefore a shout full of faith and confidence in God. It was a shout full of assurance that he would give them the victory. *How* he would do it, they had no clue, but that he would indeed do it, they were fully persuaded.

Years ago, my fellow evangelist and I were working in a very difficult place when God came to us both and, remarkably, on the same afternoon, as we waited separately before the Lord, gave us the same verse. We were certain that the Lord would work in power, but circumstances dictated that we had to leave the area fairly abruptly without seeing anything of that which we both felt God was about to do. We had believed and had the assurance of faith, but nothing came of it. We went our separate ways and about three years later we met again at a convention. We sat together and talked over our midday meal. He had just paid a visit to the area where we had been working at that time and he said to me, 'Do you remember this one and that one? Do you remember that family and this one?'

'Yes,' I answered.

'They're saved, brother,' he said. 'They simply came to the Lord after we left and they are following him today.' It was such a tender conversation. We wept together at the table as we remembered how God had spoken to us there and given such assurance to us. We had left with such heavy hearts, but now, years later, God's word to our hearts was vindicated and he had done what he told us he would do. Faith's assurance is a very precious thing.

The triumph of faith

'So the people shouted when the priests blew the trumpets. And it happened when the people heard the sound of the trumpet, and the people shouted with a great shout, that the wall fell down flat. Then the people went up into the city, every man straight before him, and they took the city' (v. 20).

It was not the fierce yell that dislodged the walls and brought them down. Regardless of the fortifications put up by the enemy, God performed the miracle. The shout was a shout of assurance and triumph in God. The time had come and God was about to step onto the scene and give victory over the most formidable obstacle of all—Jericho.

Jesus said, 'If you can believe, all things are possible to him who believes' (Mark 9:23); 'If you ask anything in my name, I will do it' (John 14:14); 'Ask, and you will receive, that your joy may be full' (John 16:24). 'Through God we will do valiantly, for it is he who shall tread down our enemies' (Psalm 60:12). Faith looks away from itself, with all its frailties and infirmities, towards a mighty God. 'And this is the victory that has overcome the world—our faith' (1 John 5:4). When faith is exercised, the world can neither enthral nor intimidate. It elevates the soul above all the elements which had weakened it. God has come to our rescue and he is the mighty Victor. Jericho is recorded for the encouragement of the saints throughout the ages.

For several centuries the longsuffering of God had waited, because 'the iniquity of the Amorites is not yet complete' (Genesis 15:16), but now the time of his wrath had come. The Canaanites were ripe for destruction and the Israelites were the instruments of judgement. God's consuming wrath was about to be expressed in the extermination of the people who embraced and practised evil.

Only Rahab was saved. The walls fell in such a way as to spare the destruction of Rahab's house. She, too, lived by faith.

The triumph put great heart into the nation of Israel. Nothing now was impossible to them, for their God was with them in power. The Canaanites in the land were demoralized. They knew their hour had come. God had come to possess the land.

Two things signalled the fall of the city: the trumpet and the shout. This reminds us of that great event soon to take place, when 'The Lord himself will descend from heaven with a shout, with the voice of an archangel, and with the trumpet of God' (1 Thes. 4:16). It's Jericho all over again, but on a much grander scale! What a day of victory this will be when we rejoice in the mighty shout of that final day of eternal victory in the presence of our God!

Notes

1 **Alan Redpath,** *Victorious Christian Living* (London: Pickering & Inglis, 1956), p. 106.
2 **Charles Wesley,** 'Father of Jesus Christ my Lord', verse 14 (1742).

The defeat at Ai (7:1–26)

Jericho was conquered through faith, courage and obedience; the causes of defeat at Ai were covetousness, disobedience, prayerlessness and self-confidence.

The chapter begins with the significant and pivotal word 'But'. The fantastic victory at Jericho was simply unbelievable. Now that this important city was demolished, Israel was on a winning streak and would just surge forward from one mighty victory to another. The shouts of triumph would echo through the land … 'But' Israel sinned! The experience of victory may blind us to the possibility of defeat. Heights are dangerous places. We are extremely vulnerable in moments of apparent success, for we are then over-confident and have the mistaken notion that we can handle things in our own strength. There are those who have been greatly used of God who have, in the flush of spiritual success, fallen badly.

Achan took 'of the accursed things' from Jericho in disobedience to the command and in defiance of the threat (6:18).

The important statement is in the first verse: 'The anger of the LORD burned against the children of Israel.' That is the real reason why they were defeated. They failed because God was angry. The wrath of God is a terrible reality before which men should tremble.

'Israel committed a trespass' or 'acted unfaithfully' (v. 1), and Israel's unfaithfulness provoked God's anger. The Israelites were to spare none and take nothing. They obeyed the first command, but Achan fell into the trap of covetousness and took that which God commanded them to leave. Although only one person acted in this unfaithful manner, all Israel was held liable. One person can be a great blessing or a curse to a community or nation. Achan was a curse. 'One sinner destroys much good' (Eccles. 9:18). Israel was a unit and when one member sinned the whole was said to have sinned. The New Testament speaks of the church as a unit. 'And if one member suffers, all the members suffer with it' (1 Corinthians 12:26). When we sin we affect others. When Achan sinned all Israel suffered. Achan means 'Trouble' and he certainly troubled Israel that day. There was sin in the camp and God was angry. God knew all about it, and sooner or later that sin would be exposed. The Israelites were allowed to be cruelly defeated in battle and that was the trigger which set the wheels of discovery and exposure in motion. The judgement of God would soon fall.

The disaster at Ai mirrors another incident on their travels. At Kadesh Barnea they failed, and when they later decided in their own strength (without the ark) to go up, they were soundly beaten (Numbers 14:39–45). History repeats itself and now, in their blatant self-confidence, again without the ark, they go up to Ai and suffer an ignominious defeat.

The New Testament parallels the Old in that both deal with wicked men: the one at the beginning of Israel's battle for Canaan and the other at the beginning of the church's ministry to the world. God was establishing the fact that purity is essential for those who follow him. Achan, at the beginning of Israel's conquest of Canaan, and Ananias, at the beginning of the church's conquest of the world, are brothers alike in guilt and doom. Joshua had to deal with Achan as Peter had to deal with Ananias (Acts 5). It was corruption from within, and that is the worst kind of opposition to have.

The preparation (vv. 2–3)

After the victory of Jericho, Joshua proceeded immediately to the next task which lay before him. He would strike while the iron was hot! He wisely, as a good military leader, sent out scouts to reconnoitre the area and spy out the town of Ai. Ai was in a strategic position for control of the hill country to the north and to the south. Joshua did not give himself to feasting and celebration. He was a dedicated soldier and an able commander.

SELF-CONFIDENCE

The spies are neither named nor given specific credentials, unlike in Numbers 13. Secondly, the spies, in their report, say or do nothing to assure Joshua that the task will succeed. Thirdly, they give no certainty of victory, unlike in Numbers 14:8 and 21:34, where it was reported that the Lord 'will bring us into this land and give it to us'. Their reliance was not on God. There was no mention of divine promises. Their evaluation and recommendation was a military strategy based on human judgement. How very different was the report of the spies who were sent to look over Jericho! They had said, 'Truly the LORD has delivered all the land into our hands' (2:24). Their confidence then was in God. These spies, however, were brimming over with self-confidence and were inflated with pride at the victory at Jericho. They contemptuously regarded Ai as easy prey. 'The people of Ai are few,' they said.

EASE-LOVING LAZINESS

Ai was on high ground north of Jerusalem. It would have meant some considerable exertion to climb twenty-four kilometres (about fifteen miles) from Gilgal, 240 metres below sea level, to about 500 metres above sea level (about 800 metres in all). So it was logical to say that it was not necessary for the whole army to toil up the mountain for so insignificant a foe. Some folk in the service of the Lord are time-servers who do what is expected of them but not much more. There is a careful and calculated giving of themselves. Being concerned about overwork in the Lord's service reflects the attitude of the flesh.

PRAYERLESSNESS

The spies then arrogantly plotted the battle strategy without reference to God or his appointed leader! This should be in the hands of deity! Did God not give the nation instructions as to how the battle against Jericho was to be fought and won? They recommended that two or three thousand men would be sufficient to overcome the insignificant town of Ai. Joshua simply accepted their recommendation and failed completely in his leadership at this point.

Ai had 12,000 inhabitants (8:25), which would probably have given a fighting force of about 2,000 men. Not only, therefore, was there self-confidence, there was also prayerlessness. Joshua failed to wait on God. He did not prostrate himself in humility before God to hear what he had to say. Rather he took the matter into his own hands and allowed the advice of the spies to prevail. Joshua, a man of such calibre who had known the presence of God and had been so greatly used, failed God. Whatever victories we have seen and however near to God we may have been, we always need to be dependent on God. We must keep close to him lest we act independently and prayerlessly.

Remember that 'the anger of the LORD burned against the children of Israel'; now God was watching their prayerless, arrogant over-confidence, knowing that they were soon to suffer an ignominious defeat at the hands of the men of Ai. They needed to be taught a lesson which would restore his leadership of the nation and cause the people to realize that without him they were helpless in the face of the enemy. God was angry.

Their humiliation (vv. 4–5)

There were no explicit divine directions, for God had not commanded them to take Ai, and there is no mention of Joshua's leadership. This situation has the ingredients of defeat. They were on untried territory.

The 3,000 Israelites advanced towards Ai, but the men of Ai put them to flight. They chased them 'as far as Shebarim'. Thirty-six men were killed. The rout was complete. 'The hearts of the people melted and became like water' (v. 5). The same expression was used of the Canaanites in 2:11, but now the tables were turned and the Israelites experienced the same terror as they faced destruction by the people of the land.

The cause of the disaster was sin. 'Israel has sinned ... Therefore the children of Israel could not stand before their enemies' (vv. 11–12). How dangerous and destructive are the effects of sin! The shameful defeat was the inevitable result of disobedience. Carnal plans were confidently accepted by human reasoning without divine guidance and divine endorsement. And behind it all, in the darkness and stealth, there was the sin of Achan eliciting God's anger.

Sin in the church is a great problem. So many churches are in a lamentable condition because of hidden sin, and instead of enjoying the blessing of the Lord, they must endure his anger. They are humiliated before the forces of evil instead of experiencing victory. A deadness prevails over one meeting after another. The presence of the Lord is rarely sensed. When last was there a conversion? The vibrancy of healthy growth is absent. There is sin in the camp—hidden carnality—and it kills the spirit of power and liberty. Until the wrong is put right there will be no spiritual progress. Sin must be dealt with or the cycle of deadness and defeat will simply continue to weaken and perhaps even destroy the fellowship.

The desperation (v. 6)

Joshua was distraught. Look at this vivid description of the leader and his elders, prostrate before the ark with rent garments, and with dust and dirt on their heads and in their hair, because of the failure and stunning defeat. How very different to some churches and fellowships today, where the reality of decline is denied and where the people refuse to recognize that the Lord is displeased! There is no seeking God for mercy but rather a false optimism and an assumption that all is well.

Joshua was shattered. This was no light problem. He faced the failure head-on. The power that had been evident at Jericho was no longer there! Failures must be faced—the problems won't go away just because we regard them as insignificant.

Notice that he fell before the ark of God that represented the presence of God. This is the first mention of the ark in this chapter. At last it is brought into the picture. At last God is acknowledged. The whole episode had been conducted without reference to the One who had given them that astounding passage across the flooded Jordan and the impossible victory over Jericho—but at last Joshua goes to God! It's a bit late to be seeking God now, but better late than never. He was on the right track—he went to God. So many turn away from him when they hit problems. Joshua took the right route.

Notice also that the elders were with him in his dismay. They did not castigate nor condemn him, as so many had done to Moses in times of trouble in the wilderness. They identified with him in his grief.

The supplication (vv. 7–9)

HIS ACCUSATION

'Why have you brought this people over the Jordan at all—to deliver us into the hand of the Amorites, to destroy us?' (v. 7). Bold words indeed! He should have remembered the words of God in Exodus 23: 'But if you indeed obey his voice and do all that I speak, then I will be an enemy to your enemies and … the Amorites … I will cut … off' (vv. 22–23). Had he not been charged to 'meditate' on and to 'observe to do' all that was written in the Book of the Law? God's promise to make their way prosperous and give them 'good success' was conditional on Joshua living in the Word (Joshua 1:8). Why then did he not take the words in Exodus 23 to heart? It would have saved him a lot of grief! The reason why the Amorites were not cut off was obviously because the Israelites had not obeyed God. The disaster at Ai was not God's fault, but Israel's.

HIS LAMENTATION

'Oh, that we had been content, and dwelt on the other side of the Jordan!' Joshua knew that he had obeyed God in crossing the Jordan and now he blames God indirectly by saying that their obedience brought them into trouble. We've heard this language before, haven't we? It was voiced at the

Red Sea: 'It would have been better for us to serve the Egyptians than that we should die in the wilderness' (Exodus 14:12); and later when they were hungry: 'Oh, that we had died by the hand of the LORD in the land of Egypt' (Exodus 16:3); and again when they were thirsty: 'Why is it you have brought us up out of Egypt, to kill us and our children and our livestock with thirst?' (Exodus 17:3); also at Kadesh Barnea: 'If only we had died in the land of Egypt! ... Let us select a leader and return to Egypt' (Numbers 14:2–4).

The unruly and dissatisfied people had vented their anger on Moses and now their dissatisfaction had entered into Joshua's own heart; he who had seen so much of God's mighty power now took up their very words in a heart-rending complaint against the God whom he had served so well. Beware lest the spirit of bitterness enter your own soul and pour forth to your own detriment and to the confusion and hurt of others. Carnal thinking invents many strange reasons for defeats.

HIS CONFUSION

'O Lord, what shall I say when Israel turns its back before its enemies?' (v. 8). Joshua is bewildered at this sudden and shameful turn of events after the mighty victories at Jordan and Jericho. In this period of humiliation, some rays of faith emerge. He recognizes that God had brought them over the Jordan (v. 7). His statement that Israel should never turn their back on their enemies (v. 8) suggests that he knows that God's people should experience victory. He has concern for God's great name (v. 9). It is faith struggling to come to terms with the humiliation of defeat and the horror of anticipated annihilation. Where is God in all of this? Has he broken his covenant with them? Has God forsaken them—and why? His bold and strong language reflects his desperation in incomprehensible circumstances. Joshua is struggling to find sense in the disaster. His faith is groping for an answer as he attempts to understand. He still knows nothing of Achan's sin and is confused and distraught.

HIS TREPIDATION

'For the Canaanites and all the inhabitants of the land will hear it, and surround us, and cut off our name from the earth' (v. 9). Yes, they will most certainly hear of it and will unite to annihilate Israel. Joshua faced the bleakest of prospects. His was a perfectly reasonable forecast. When God's people disobey him and live badly, the world thinks ill of them. They are scorned as hypocrites by those who know that they should be different. Their worldliness and shallowness betray the One whom they claim to serve and they have no testimony in the community. The Canaanites—the worldlings—will be entrenched in their evil practices because the lives of those who are defeated and failing carry neither conviction nor rebuke.

HIS MOTIVATION

'Then what will you do for your great name?' The prayer is blunt, simple and to the point. Joshua did not plead the promises or form pious phrases. This defeat could bring great reproach and contempt upon God. If Israel's name were to be wiped off the face of the earth, what would happen to God's great name? It was the honour of God that was at stake. He was concerned for the divine glory. He could not bear to think of God being reduced to an object of scorn and contempt. This is the noblest point of Joshua's prayer.

God's condemnation (vv. 10–12)

THE CALL TO ACTION

Joshua's prayer is not offensive to God. He does not condemn Joshua for his strong words, for they have a kind of honesty, openness and transparency. Nevertheless he almost rebukes Joshua for praying at all ('Why do you lie thus on your face?' v. 10), for this problem is not to be solved by prayer but by taking active steps to cast out the unclean thing. God is angry with the sin in which they are all corporately involved. The sin of one has had a profound effect upon the whole community. What is done in private has public effect, 'for none of us lives to himself' (Romans 14:7). God is dealing with them as a corporate body. No man can tell how far the blight of his secret sins may reach. No individual Christian can sin without affecting the whole church. 'Israel has sinned.' The whole nation has been infected. What a salutary lesson!

God now rebukes Joshua and commands him to 'Get up!' The time for prayer and mourning is gone. God takes sin seriously, and it must now be discovered and removed. 'Joshua, don't grieve for the defeat; eliminate the cause.' We have such tame views of sin today. We have been conditioned to sin in society and it has become acceptable. We just use other names to describe it and overlook so much. Sin is excused on every hand, but, call it what you will, in God's eyes it is evil and it needs to be exposed and judged. 'Get up! The time for mourning is over; the time for exposure has come!'

THEIR CONDUCT ANALYSED

'Israel has sinned, and they have also transgressed my covenant which I commanded them. For they have even taken some of the accursed things, and have both stolen and deceived; and they have also put it among their own stuff' (v. 11). God's detailed description of Achan's sin is revealing. He describes the sin in six different ways: the first three are with regard to God and the next three with regard to men. He says that Israel sinned, transgressed and disobeyed, and also that they stole, deceived and concealed.

- *Sin* means to miss the mark. It was seen to be deliberate, with the idea of personal responsibility.
- *Transgression* here means to pass over or to pass by. God had commanded that they take nothing from Jericho, and they simply passed by the command.
- *Disobedience*. They deliberately disobeyed God's instructions.
- *Stealing*. God had said, 'All the silver and gold … shall come into the treasury of the LORD' (6:19). Achan stole from God. Malachi says plainly, 'You have robbed me!' (Malachi 3:8). He took that which was

consecrated to God. Many are sinning against him by withholding that which is rightfully his.

- *Deceiving.* Achan deceived the people until forced to admit his crime.
- *Concealment.* Achan thought that no one at all would ever know!
- *Trespass* (v. 1). The Hebrew word here means 'treachery'. Achan was a traitor—unfaithful to his commander and to his Lord. Some are unfaithful in their ministry and in their walk with God—it's treachery!
- *Folly* or *disgrace.* Achan thought that he was clever. No one knew! But sin is foolish and brings disgrace.

THE THREAT PRONOUNCED

In his analysis God brings the argument to a chilling close. Because Israel sinned they were defeated and 'doomed to destruction' (v. 12). God's judgement is clear: 'Neither will I be with you anymore, unless you destroy the accursed from among you.' That is about as serious as it can get. There is nothing worse than the divine withdrawal. 'I will return again to my place till they acknowledge their offence' (Hosea 5:15). 'Without me', said Jesus, 'you can do nothing' (John 15:5). The presence of God is everything! How often our meetings are barren, dry, cold, without conviction and with no sense of the presence of the Lord! Amazingly, many don't discern that it is so! They are content to allow things to continue in this arid state. Should they not be asking why God does not flood the atmosphere any more? Why he has withdrawn his presence? What a threat! The divine withdrawal! Nothing is more crucial than the presence of God with his people (1:5,9; 3:7,10; 4:14; 6:27). To forfeit that is disaster.

'Please, God, don't forsake us and leave us to our own devices. Have mercy, Lord! Please reveal the corruption and cleanse it away—and then return, return, return, O our holy and wonderful Lord.'

God's instruction (vv. 13–18)

The first 'Get up' (v. 10) was a rebuke; the second 'Get up' (v. 13) was to institute the divine inquisition. The sin must be found! God then gives instructions for the investigation. God hates sin!

God's innate character is holiness: 'I am holy' (1 Peter 1:16). The only way in which we can have fellowship with him is in his holiness. It is there and only there that God imparts his holy presence. In his righteousness and holiness he must condemn sin, but in his love he has provided the means for cleansing from that sin. Holiness is the central theme of the whole Bible. Without it the character of God is destroyed and the whole plan of salvation is unnecessary, for sinful living would then be the accepted norm. Holiness should be central to the proclamation of the Word in every pulpit. Holiness should be the watchword of every Christian. Sin has invaded our lives as a dominating tyrant, as an inward enemy, as a moral corruption, as a spiritual sickness. Its devastating results are evident on every hand. It has broken hearts and broken homes. It is a defiling, repulsive filthiness which tears families and fellowships apart. There is nothing nice about sin. It may dress itself up to be attractive, desirable and necessary, but its end is destruction and sorrow.

Amazingly, the emphasis in much of today's preaching is not on sin and holiness. That would not be popular. Some would be offended and would withdraw from the church. So the message is toned down and the emphasis is placed on acceptable topics. Positive aspects of the deeper life are emphasized, but the hurtful element of sin in the believer is sidestepped, for it would cause too much disruption and might lose the preacher his acceptance and popularity.

Today's popular emphasis is on sensationalism, signs and wonders and the like—and the heart of the message is left virtually untouched. A penetrating analysis and condemnation of sin and wickedness would be unthinkable. The tide of evil floods the land, and the church raises but a whimper against it. To preach on holiness would, in some places, almost empty the church. Yet God's unchangeable law still stands: 'You shall be holy, for I the LORD your God am holy' (Leviticus 19:2).

In this story of Achan, we see that sin brought a whole nation to a point of disaster. Corruption in the church does the damage. Treacherous Israelites are to be dreaded more than malicious Canaanites. The nation must be investigated, sin must be located and judgement must be executed. The evil must be purged from their midst! 'Be sure your sin will find you out' (Numbers 32:23). God revealed the sin of Joseph's brothers, of David's murder and adultery, of Ananias and Sapphira's greed and deceit, of Adam and Eve's disobedience. We cannot escape the all-seeing eye of God. 'All things are naked and open to the eyes of him to whom we must give account' (Hebrews 4:13).

THE PROCEDURE WAS EXTENSIVE

'In the morning therefore you shall be brought according to your tribes. And it shall be that the tribe which the LORD takes shall come according to families …' (v. 14). There must be no delay in dealing with the evil — 'in the morning'. However hurtful it may be, all Israel must be thoroughly investigated. They all share the shame. Not taking drastic action will cause those outside to conclude that we approve of the sin which brought the defeat. It must be discovered and eliminated, however wide the search.

THE PROCEDURE WAS INCLUSIVE

It included not only the tribes in general, but families and individuals in particular. None shall escape. 'Search me, O God, and know my heart … and see if there is any wicked way in me' (Psalm 139:23–24). Be willing to know the worst as he searches and exposes. Submit to his dealing. Let God pursue everything which is displeasing to him. Let nothing escape! Don't hide that sin scurrying into the dark corners of your heart. Whatever it costs in terms of humiliation and reputation, seek out that Achan in your soul and have done with it forever. Is it still there after all that God has done for you? Is that cringing, cowering, protesting Achan still there? For the sake of the health of your soul, and for the sake of the whole body of Christ, be honest and confess the presence of this evil thing. Secret sins affect others. Go alone with God and open all the areas of your heart to his penetrating gaze; then let him pass the sentence, deal with it in judgement and with you in restoration.

Achan must have felt quite secure in the thought that Israel was a large nation and it was not likely that he would be discovered. Sin hides well! But in the search, the tribe of Judah was taken. Then the family of the Zarhites was taken. Achan's heart must have skipped a beat as he saw the net closing in. Horrors—Zabdi was taken! And then they came forward man by man, and Achan was taken. The process of elimination was complete; the sin was pin-pointed. What a humiliating moment of shame and disgrace! May God grant that in our own hearts, when the Achan is discovered, it will be a moment of broken-hearted repentance, confession, forgiveness, cleansing and restoration.

THE PROCEDURE WAS EXPULSIVE

They were told to 'take away the accursed thing from among you' (v. 13). There is a ray of hope in God's dealings here, for he says, 'Neither will I be with you anymore, unless you destroy the accursed from among you' (v. 12). The possibility of reconciliation with God was seen in his prescribed road to recovery—'*unless*'. The only way that their journey could be resumed in victory and triumph was if the evil were removed. Judgement would have to be meted out, *then* God could be with them again. Judgement is tinged with grace. In wrath, God remembers mercy.

The investigation (v. 19)

Achan saw the disaster that he had brought upon Israel but he was not driven by remorse to repent. He clung to his ill-gotten gains as long as he could and concealed his guilt until he could no longer hide his sin, thus adding to his guilt. His was no tender conscience. There was no voluntary confession. He was given many opportunities to confess his sin but he remained silent. Did his conscience not trouble him when he saw that thirty-six lives had been lost? Achan's resistant attitude and hard heart were seen by the whole nation through the process of elimination. They might have had pity had Joshua told them who the culprit was and that he had repented, but the extensive public search revealed Achan's true heart and sealed his fate.

Joshua speaks with kind fatherly care: 'My son, I beg you …' Using the term 'my son' means that he is speaking not only in fatherly terms, but also as a senior and superior to a junior.

'Give glory to the LORD God of Israel …' Confessing wrong confirms the law and honours God. It reveals the evil of our deeds and the righteousness of God. It establishes the law and vindicates the character and justice of God. It gives glory to God.

'Make confession to him, and tell me now what you have done.' Achan had to confess it. It was a personal issue and had to be *personally* dealt with. It is not 'we have sinned', but 'I have sinned'. Confession is not to be in general terms but must be specific. All sin must be confessed to God and to those whom we have wronged by our sins; therefore Achan had to confess it not only to God, but also to Joshua as representative of the whole of Israel against whom he had sinned.

It also had to be confessed 'now'. Delayed confessions only prolong grief and heartache, and delay solving the problems. There was to be *immediacy*.

'Do not hide it from me.' There had to be *honesty* and integrity in the confession. Nothing was to be hidden. He had been hiding it long enough, but now he must come clean. Partial or general confessions will never do. Some people confess superficially in order to conceal their true state, but this will never solve the heart's problem. All must be brought out into the open before the eyes of him with whom we have to do.

The confession (vv. 20–21)

Joshua invited Achan to make his confession. It was extracted under compulsion and made too late for mercy. It would but condemn him. But he was so devastatingly honest.

And Achan answered Joshua and said, 'Indeed I have sinned against the LORD God of Israel, and this is what I have done: When I saw among the spoils a beautiful Babylonian garment, two hundred shekels of silver, and a wedge of gold weighing fifty shekels, I coveted them and took them. And there they are, hidden in the earth in the midst of my tent, with the silver under it.'

'I saw … I coveted … I took … I hid.'

THE ADMISSION OF HIS SIN

Achan's confession, made under duress, did not indicate contrition. He was sorry that he had been caught, not sorry that he sinned. He acknowledged his guilt and wrongdoing, but this was no more an indication of contrition than King Saul's admission when he did not obey God in the matter of the Amalekites: 'I have sinned' (1 Samuel 15:24); or the remorseful wail of Judas: 'I have sinned by betraying innocent blood' (Matthew 27:4).

THE ENORMITY OF HIS SIN

He had sinned 'against the LORD God of Israel'. He eventually recognized that this was what he had done. David cried out, 'Against you, you only, have I sinned, and done this evil in your sight' (Psalm 51:4). When we sin we may hurt and damage others, but chiefly our sin is against God. In our sin we turn from that love and act independently. Spurned love is exceedingly painful. Do you ever think of the pain it brings to God when we sin?

THE ADVANCE OF HIS SIN

Achan 'saw', Eve 'saw' (Genesis 3:6), the sons of God 'saw' (Genesis 6:2),

David 'saw' (2 Samuel 11:2). Achan must have been mesmerized. The psalmist said, 'Turn away my eyes from looking at worthless things' (Psalm 119:37). Job said, 'I have made a covenant with my eyes' (Job 31:1). The eye-gate must be guarded constantly and carefully. We cannot always prevent seeing evil, but if we dwell on it we open the door to sin.

THE ATTRACTIVENESS OF THE SIN

Achan saw a 'beautiful Babylonian garment', and he lusted after this and the silver and gold. Sin attracts and allures; it fascinates and fools; it draws and damns. We must have it. It becomes an obsession.

So it was with Achan. He could withstand it no longer. He saw and he coveted. The consequences of being disobedient faded into the background. That which was before him he had to have. It became a force which he could not control. 'He who is greedy for gain troubles his own house' (Proverbs 15:27), and that day Achan brought great trouble to his house. He was greedy for gain and disobeyed God in order to get it. All kinds of devices are invented, all kinds of twisted plans are devised to grasp the things the heart desires. 'But those who desire to be rich fall into temptation and a snare, and into many foolish and harmful lusts which drown men in destruction and perdition' (1 Timothy 6:9).

THE ACT OF SIN

Greed had burned within him and now it led to action. He 'took' that which he so desired. The gold and silver had to be given to God and the garment had to be burnt with the rest of the city, but those commands were vague and distant now that he had the garment and the gold in his hands. He could no longer resist the powerful urge and he stole them. What a thief sin is! It stole Achan's character, it robbed God's work, it brought great distress and defeat to God's people, it dishonoured God, it killed thirty-six men and it halted the advance of the people of God. Sin always has consequences.

THE SECRECY OF SIN

No sooner had he gained possession of his plunder than it became his burden. He had to hide it, and this he did in his tent, involving all those who lived with him there. He made the mistake which so many make: he thought that his sin would never be found out. He could sin and get away with it. But your sin will be found out, however secure you might imagine yourself to be. You will be discovered.

The examination (vv. 22–23)

IT WAS WISE

The court ruling did not depend on Achan's testimony alone. They had to investigate his confession. Before judgement could be pronounced, everyone had to be certain of the guilt of the accused. No one in the future would be able to complain that judgement was meted out in error. The facts must be clearly set out before all.

IT WAS RAPID

Immediately, Joshua sent messengers and 'they ran to the tent'. There were no delays or adjournments for lengthy periods. Joshua conducted a good court.

IT WAS CONCLUSIVE

'And they took them from the midst of the tent, brought them to Joshua and to all the children of Israel, and laid them out before the LORD.' All the exhibits were laid out in the open for all to see. The evidence was conclusive. Achan was guilty. Here again is a warning that it is futile to attempt to hide anything from the God whose eyes 'are in every place, keeping watch on the evil and the good' (Proverbs 15:3).

The execution (vv. 24–26)

Now that the culprit had been found and proved guilty, it was time for the execution.

THE PLACE

It has been suggested that the Buqeiah Valley could fit the boundary description of 15:7. If it is the Buqeiah Valley, the journey from Jericho would have been about thirteen kilometres (eight miles), emphasizing the concern to remove the impurity from Israel's midst.

Here it is called the Valley of Achor. Achor means 'trouble', as does the word Achan. Joshua said that if anyone took of the accursed things he would 'trouble' Israel (6:18), and now Achan has become the 'Troubler of Israel'—some title! Sin troubles the church, and there are those in the church who trouble it because they have not yet done with sin.

THE PRONOUNCEMENT

Joshua uses the words for trouble again. He says, 'Why have you troubled us? The LORD will trouble you this day' (v. 25). Achan even gave his name to the valley of execution, for it certainly was a valley of trouble.

THE PUNISHMENT

'All Israel stoned him with stones; and they burned them with fire after they had stoned them with stones.' It was not only Achan who suffered but also his family and all that he had. That the goods had been buried in his tent meant that the whole family knew about the incident and consequently bore the same punishment. Why did they not say anything when the search was being conducted? They kept silent and increased their guilt, so judgement fell on the whole family.

The punishment was severe. Achan had not reckoned with the holiness of God. God would not tolerate disobedience, especially if that disobedience led to the defeat of Israel at the hands of those whom they had been sent to punish for their iniquities. Thirty-six men had lost their lives, and Israel and her God had been put to shame before the nations. No, Achan's sin was great, and he would have to pay for it in the most severe way possible.

At the opening of the tabernacle worship there was recorded an instance of the severity of God's judgement upon the two sons of Aaron (Leviticus 10:1–2). At the beginning of the church Ananias and Sapphira were likewise judged (Acts 5); now here at the entry into the land of Canaan we have a further execution of God's severe judgement. At the beginning of each new era godly living was promoted and wickedness warned against.

Here is also a revelation of divine discipline. How lax is that discipline in many churches today, where a blind eye is turned to sin of all kinds, and those of ability, however far they are from the Lord, are sometimes placed in positions of authority! The church can but suffer and fail to progress when sin is tolerated.

THE MEMORIAL HEAP OF STONES

'Then they raised over him a great heap of stones.' The first pile of stones was raised in the river Jordan, and the next on the banks of the Jordan as a prominent memorial to the miraculous crossing of the river. This is the third heap of stones, and this one is a memorial to the intensity of God's hatred of sin and to the severity of God's judgement on sin. It was a terrible warning to those who imagined themselves to be secure in their secret sin. We must never deal leniently with sin. We need ever to hold high the holiness of the God whom we serve.

THE RECONCILIATION

'So the LORD turned from the fierceness of his anger.' The last verse in this chapter counteracts the first verse, where we read, 'The anger of the LORD burned against the children of Israel.' Now that sin has been dealt with, God and his people are reconciled again. They are restored to his favour and blessing.

Hosea gives an additional and beautiful ending to this story: 'I will give her … the Valley of Achor as a door of hope' (Hosea 2:15). Where the work of execution is faithfully performed there is a door of hope! Isaiah adds to this: 'The Valley of Achor [shall be] a place for herds to lie down, for my people who have sought me' (Isaiah 65:10). In restoration and communion with the Lord there is hope for all the future, and satisfaction in the knowledge of the blessedness of his presence.

Victory at Ai (8:1–35)

N
ow that the sin had been removed, Israel was able to progress.
Discipline had been applied and the nation was once again ready
for action. So many refrain from discipline because of the price of
the pain and disruption it causes, but then they reap the consequences—no
progress, and the distress and bitterness of carnal wranglings.

Joshua did not know whether his action against Achan was acceptable
to God and whether there would be further requirements before
communion with him could be restored. He could have been disheartened
with all the recent events and have been 'swallowed up with too much
sorrow' (2 Corinthians 2:7), but God, mindful of his servant's needs,
stepped in with a wonderful word of encouragement, cheer and promise:
'Do not be afraid ...' (vv. 1–2).

In this chapter we see the following:
• God reassures Joshua (vv. 1–2).
• Joshua gives instructions concerning the ambush (vv. 3–9).
• Joshua and the army go up to Ai (vv. 10–13).
• Ai is left unguarded as the men from Ai are drawn out (vv. 14–17).
• God directs the battle (v. 18).
• The ambush is carried out (vv. 19–20).
• Joshua and his regiments turn back on the men of Ai (vv. 21–23).
• Ai is destroyed (vv. 24–29).
• An altar is built and offerings made (vv. 30–31).
• The covenant is renewed near Shechem (vv. 32–35).

The encouragement (vv. 1– 2)
The fact that God says to Joshua, 'Arise' (v. 1) may well indicate that
Joshua was on his knees or on his face before God, chastened in spirit after

the fall. God now gives him the wonderful reassurance that he is with his people.

THERE IS A WORD OF COMFORT

'Do not be afraid, nor be dismayed' (v. 1). God's earlier promises of divine assistance had been jeopardized by the Israelites' disobedience, but now this problem had been dealt with. Joshua and the people of God were now in need of reassurance that they had been restored to God's favour and that they could depend on his leading. Was God with them now? They would have been apprehensive and fearful.

Don't be despondent after a defeat and conclude that victory will never come. 'Do not rejoice over me, my enemy; when I fall, I will arise' (Micah 7:8). Turn the failure to good account. Satan sometimes oversteps his mark and, although he may have won a battle, he is not in control and even the failure can be a stepping-stone to higher things.

My friend David's brother Jan was the champion heavyweight boxer of his university. On one occasion his university met another in a boxing tournament. Each university won three fights and the outcome rested on the final heavyweight engagement in which Jan was to fight. They entered the ring and both fought well, being fairly evenly matched. 'Suddenly,' said Jan, 'I found myself on the canvas, hearing in disbelief the referee counting me out. I struggled to my feet before the count ended and remembered one vital instruction from my trainer: "If he knocks you down, he will come in for the kill. Then you must unleash everything you have and give him the shock of his life." He came at me, and I just let rip.' At once the fight was reversed and to cheering crowds, Jan went on to win comfortably. He won, the tournament was won, the university won. He was the hero of the hour. But what would have happened if he had said, 'Oh dear, the count is five, six, seven … I'll never make it; I may as well lie here and be counted out, for I have no chance against this formidable opponent'? Had he said that he would have lost, the tournament would have been lost, the university would have lost. But Jan rose from the seeming defeat. He did not lie there in despair. He got up! He faced the opponent, and turned apparent defeat into glorious victory.

Don't let defeat ruin your life. Get up! The secret of going on is getting up! Jan trusted in the advice of his trainer and won the day. We have a greater word from a greater Trainer. He speaks forgiveness and reassurance to our saddened hearts. He says, 'Do not be afraid, nor be dismayed … Arise, go …' He assures us that he has not cast us aside, but will give us strength to rise from the ashes and conquer. 'He restores my soul' (Psalm 23:3).

'Do not be afraid, nor be dismayed.' It was a word from God. The way to get back into a fully functioning, confident relationship with God is to get a word from him. If you want to overcome your feeling of failure after a defeat you must get into the Word of God and hear from him. As we claim his word, he plants it in our hearts. 'Strengthen me according to your word' (Psalm 119:28). 'If we confess our sins, he is faithful and just to forgive us our sins and to cleanse us from all unrighteousness' (1 John 1:9). Oh, the comfort of the Word of God!

THERE IS A WORD OF INSTRUCTION

'Take all the people of war with you, and arise, go up to Ai.' The time for action had come. Joshua must now turn from the throne of God to the field of service. Previously but 3,000 men had gone, but now God says, 'Take all the people of war.' This word came as a rebuke. He did not have to be reminded again, for in all the future battles in Canaan he took all the men of war with him! All were to be involved. When we attempt a project for God, all the church should be involved, not just the faithful, willing few. There is great value in full participation. It will cost effort and all must be willing to give freely of their energies, abilities and substance to that effort. We should not underestimate the power of the enemy.

THERE IS A WORD OF STRATEGY

'Lay an ambush.' The strategy was humbling. They had to hide away behind Ai instead of triumphantly marching round the city as they had done at Jericho. God does not always work in the same way. Having won one victory we cannot presume to use the same methods in the next battle. On this occasion Joshua would come against the city and make as though he was fleeing before the men of Ai, who would come out against them as before. When they had left the city the men in ambush would then rise and take the city, surrounding the men of Ai. This was God's plan, and they obeyed it to the letter.

Despite the fact that they had the promise of God that he would give them the city and its land, they had actively to be engaged in the conflict. God's promises are not given for us to conclude that the results are secure and that we have nothing more to do. Faith is no substitute for hard work. Hope does not absolve us of our obligations but inspires us to perform better. Our 'labour is not in vain in the Lord' (1 Corinthians 15:58). 'Take up the whole armour of God … and … stand' (Ephesians 6:13).

THERE IS A WORD OF PROMISE

'See, I have given into your hand the king of Ai, his people, his city, and his land.'

How blessed is that word from God; how wonderfully assuring; what certainty it brings. Why, when he has spoken, you can go through fire and water. You can endure all indignities, all rejections, all hardships. You can go to the uttermost part of the earth, for he is with you. He has spoken, and that puts steel into your soul. He is strengthening you to accomplish all that he has whispered to you. His word to you is the enablement for his programme for you.

THERE IS A WORD OF REWARD

'Its spoil and its cattle you shall take as booty for yourselves.' In the battle for Jericho, the gold and the silver had to be given to God, but here the spoils of the conquest were theirs. Poor Achan, he could have had his fill of all the treasures of Ai had he but waited. Achan could not wait for God's will and time, and his life ended in disaster. So many cannot wait and they try to open doors which they feel would be so beneficial—and it may not be of God at all! If only they waited; so much more is in the heart of God for them just around the corner. If God closes one door, surely he has another of greater opportunity just out of sight. Patience, patience—wait for God to show you his way. Trust him; he'll not fail you!

The exhortation and instructions (vv. 3–8)

Joshua now gave basic instructions to the men of Israel. He chose 30,000 'mighty men of valour' and sent them away by night to hide on the west side of Ai. They were specially *selected* for their trustworthiness, bravery and special abilities. So it is with Christian service: God charges those who have special qualifications to do special tasks. We can spoil the possibilities of our being chosen for front-line ministry by not living as God wants us to live and by not seeking the highest. We don't want to disqualify ourselves from special projects by living on a low spiritual level, do we?

The men were sent away by night. That meant self-sacrifice and *self-denial*. Jesus said, 'If anyone desires to come after me, let him deny himself, and take up his cross, and follow me' (Matthew 16:24). To be a good soldier there must be self-denial. The command of God may well cut across the desires of the flesh. Do you ever think of Calvary? Why, Jesus left heaven's glory. Now that was some self-denial, and all for our salvation. Will we not give ourselves unreservedly as his body here on earth to be used for the salvation of others? It may cost—but we are bound to him for his service, cost what it may.

Joshua and 5,000 men would approach the city and then retreat before the men of Ai, who would think that the Israelites were fleeing before them as before. The Israelites would draw the men of Ai out, and then the 30,000 hidden Israelites would arise from the ambush and take and burn the city. They would then come upon the men of Ai from behind and together with Joshua's men surround the men of Ai and destroy them. The instructions were precise and detailed. *Obedience* to God's commands is essential to spiritual accomplishment. *Submission*, in both military and spiritual terms, is essential for success.

A further lesson is that they were to act together. There had to be *unity*. They were not to go their separate ways but were to be led as a unit. There were to be no quarrels as to which would be the best way to go about this battle. They were to co-operate together with the united purpose of defeating the enemy. What a spirit of envy and jealousy prevails in some of our churches! 'Why should he or she be given this important task, when I can do it far better?' Self reveals itself in all its ugliness and jarring discord. Only self-crucifixion will bring wholehearted co-operation, unity, fellowship and support, and deliver the desired victory.

All was to be done 'according to the commandment of the LORD' (v. 8). At the end of this battle they were still doing everything 'according to the word of the LORD which he had commanded Joshua' (v. 27). Joshua was under God's orders and so were they all. That guaranteed success. If they continued as God had instructed, he would fulfil his wonderful *promise* and assurance: 'The LORD your God will deliver it [the city] into your hand' (v. 7). God was fighting for them. That did not exempt them from fighting—confidence in God does not produce passivity—but God's word gave them such confidence to know that he was on their side and that they would prevail.

They were all to 'be ready' (v. 4). Soldiers in any army are always to be in a state of *readiness* lest they be unexpectedly overpowered. We too are always to be ready 'lest Satan should take advantage of us' (2 Corinthians 2:11). We are to be alert and ready to fulfil God's every command—always.

'When you have taken the city ... you shall set the city on fire' (v. 8).

They were to reduce the city to ashes *immediately*. When we know what God expects of us we are to do it without hesitation. Slowness to obey God's commands is often a form of disobedience. Smoke rising from the city would cause the king of Ai to panic, realizing that the battle was lost, but would indicate to Joshua and his men that the city was taken. 'I made haste, and did not delay to keep your commandments' (Psalm 119:60).

The execution of the battle (vv. 9–29)

The moment had come and the army was sent to take up their positions behind Ai. The trap was set. Geographically speaking, the place where they hid has been described as a wild entanglement of hills and valleys, with recesses in which those waiting in ambush could hide. Nevertheless, the king of Ai should have been far more alert and should have posted sentries at various points. He was puffed up in his victory, and, to his great loss, did not do so.

'Joshua lodged that night among the people' (v. 9). He was taking nothing for granted, instructing his men in every detail. This time there must be no mistake. 'Early in the morning' Joshua mustered his people and went up before the people of Ai, who, because it was so early, did not bother to look for an ambush as they watched Joshua's advancing hordes with mounting excitement. 'They're coming again! We'll send them packing once more!'

The men of Ai were drawn out of the city and 'went out against Israel to battle' (v. 14). But the king 'did not know that there was an ambush against him'. Joshua feigned defeat and fled before the men of Ai in cowardly disarray. This was a humbling thing for him to do. Joshua and his men turned tail and ran before the men of Ai, luring them out of the city. 'They pursued Joshua and were drawn away from the city' (v. 16), and in their frantic eagerness to attack Israel, they left the city wide open. Oh, what folly!

God now takes practical control: 'He said to Joshua, "Stretch out the spear that is in your hand toward Ai, for I will give it into your hand." And Joshua stretched out the spear that was in his hand toward the city' (v. 18). It all happened as God had said it would. The ambush arose promptly, entered the city, took it and immediately set it on fire. The full reality of what had happened dawned upon the men of Ai as the smoke rose in the sky. They had nowhere to go, for Joshua's men turned from fleeing before them and began to fight. Those who had sacked the city poured out and attacked them from behind. The men of Ai were caught in the middle and were destroyed by Joshua and his armies.

The conquest was complete. They destroyed all the people in the city of Ai and took the booty. They killed all the men of Ai against whom they had fought outside the city. They took the king of Ai alive and brought him to Joshua, who hanged him on a tree until evening and then had him cut down. His corpse was thrown down at the entrance of the city where the conflict with Ai was first joined, and a great heap of stones was raised over him. There was no possibility of denying the total defeat of the city of Ai. Similarly, God wants us to have complete victory over all that is wicked and sinful. It must all be utterly destroyed. We must be cleansed from all that grieves his heart.

Notice, firstly, that God gave the word instructing them in the battle, therefore it was God who was responsible for the victory. Secondly, Joshua won because he believed the word of God and was obedient to it. The literal execution of God's word was the key to the mission's success. Thirdly, this was a miraculous victory, as was that at the Red Sea. In fact, there are several points of comparison with that event: Moses was instructed to 'lift up your rod, and stretch out your hand' (Exodus 14:16), and God said to Joshua, 'Stretch out the spear that is in your hand' (8:18). As a result of their following these instructions, Israel was victorious in both cases. The hand or arm of Moses symbolized strength or power in the dividing and later the returning of the waters. The hand of Joshua symbolized the same, for 'Joshua did not draw back his hand, with which he stretched out the spear, until he had utterly destroyed all the inhabitants of Ai' (v. 26). The staff of Moses was the symbol of his ministry, guiding the Israelites through the desert, while the sword of Joshua was the symbol of the task given to him as he conquered the land.

The Israelites were given permission to take the cattle for themselves (v. 2). The manna had stopped and now they had to fend for themselves, so this was a very welcome provision for their needs.

Israel now occupied the strategic region of Bethel and Ai, and was poised to launch its attacks both south and north.

The people of the land had sinned and the cup of their iniquity was filled to the brim: 'For all these abominations the men of the land have done … and thus the land is defiled' (Leviticus 18:27). The judgement meted out to them was therefore a consequence of their having indulged in that which displeased God intensely. His wrath rested upon those who were living in sin, and at last justice had caught up with them. They were judged by Almighty God.

The establishment of the covenant (vv. 30–35)
THE PLACE—MOUNT GERIZIM AND MOUNT EBAL (SHECHEM)

Moses had given clear instructions in Deuteronomy 11:26–32. He had said that 'you will cross over the Jordan' (v. 31). All the law that God had given him was to be remembered and recorded at a special ceremony and at a special place in the Promised Land which he named. The place was Mount Gerizim and Mount Ebal (v. 29). It is even more plainly stated in Deuteronomy 27:1–8, where Moses instructed that they were to set up large stones, whitewash them and write upon them the law of God. This was to be done at Mount Ebal. Blessings and curses were to be read out: blessings on Mount Gerizim and curses on Mount Ebal (Deuteronomy 27–28).

The distance from Ai to Shechem, which is between Gerizim and Ebal, is about fifty kilometres (thirty miles). Here the law of *Yahweh* was to be set up. Joshua would want to establish the law of God as early as possible before even the subjugation of the people of the land. There must have been panic in Canaan when they heard of Jericho and Ai being reduced to heaps of blackened ruins, and no Canaanite king would have dared to venture upon a conflict with Israel as they journeyed to Gerizim and Ebal to worship their God, even though the north had not yet been conquered. Thus God protected his people. Moreover, Shechem had no king, as we may gather from the list of thirty-one kings who were defeated by Joshua (ch. 12). The way was open for Joshua to obey the command of God through Moses and establish God's law among the people.

The twenty-four kilometres (fifteen miles) from Gilgal (about 240 metres below sea level) to Ai (about 500 metres above sea level) was quite a climb. Fifty kilometres (thirty miles) to the north and also on high ground were Mounts Gerizim and Ebal (both around 1,000 metres above sea level at their highest points). Slightly to the east and almost between them was Shechem, virtually at the centre of the country. This was the spot to which Moses had directed them to reaffirm their commitment to *Yahweh*.

The valley between these two mountains is beautiful. Where the two mountains face each other and touch most closely, with a green valley of 450 metres between, each is hollowed out, and the limestone stratum is broken into a succession of ledges. Thus a natural amphitheatre is formed, capable of containing a vast congregation of people and probably with excellent acoustic properties.

THE PURPOSE—WORSHIP

'Now Joshua built an altar to the LORD God of Israel' (v. 30). The Authorized Version translates this as: '*Then* Joshua built an altar'; after all the massive battles, they turned to worship.

Immediately after crossing the Jordan they unexpectedly stopped to institute the Passover and circumcision. Here again we are taken by surprise, for in the midst of mighty campaigns, the nation takes time off to worship their God. Should plans not immediately be made for them to forge ahead and penetrate into the heart of the country? Oh no! We find them taking this arduous journey to an appointed place for an extended period of divine worship. It is a remarkable instance of the zeal of Israel for God and for his honour. What a high priority God places on close communion with himself! He had commanded that they go there to meet him. In the hurly burly of active ministry we must never lose sight of that which God regards as most important—worship.

The altar was to be 'of whole stones over which no man has wielded an iron tool' (v. 31). The altar was the place of slaughter, of sacrifice. Its naked, simple, unadorned stones emphasized the common and ordinary state of the One who came as the meeting-place between God and man. We need much cutting and shaping, but there were no rough or sharp edges in the life of Christ. The stones were unhewn.

The altar was erected on Mount Ebal. It was on Mount Gerizim that the blessings of the Lord were to be pronounced and we should expect to find the altar there, for on Mount Ebal the curses were published (Deuteronomy 11:29). The altar was for sinners under the curse. The altar was built and the offering given on Mount Ebal, prefiguring the One who came to enter the place of the curse. The types merge, for not only is Christ the Altar, he is also the Sacrifice; he bore the curses of God for taking our sin upon himself.

The people offered burnt offerings and sacrificed peace offerings. The voluntary *burnt offering* was to be altogether consumed on the altar, signifying total surrender. This Jesus did when he went to Calvary. He held nothing back, but gave himself unreservedly as an offering for our redemption. And this is what we must do when we come to him and give our all. It indicates complete consecration.

The *peace offering* was not wholly consumed by the fire. A part was eaten by those who brought the offering, to signify that they had fellowship and communion with God. They fed on the sacrificial lamb. We too feed on the Lamb of God. They were given instructions concerning this offering: 'You shall offer peace offerings, and shall eat there, and rejoice before the LORD your God' (Deuteronomy 27:7). What wonder—how amazing! They ate and rejoiced at the place of the curse! Jesus took the curse for us—was slain—yet in this terrible offering we rejoice, for it is for our salvation. We take the life of the sacrificial Lamb who died, but who lives, and in his life which he gives to us, we live! We feed on him who is our life. Gratefully and humbly we rejoice at the place called Calvary—the place of the curse—where our sins are judged and removed and where we feast on the life of the risen Lord.

A thousand years later the Samaritans built their altar on Mount Gerizim, not Mount Ebal. The woman of Samaria pointed to Mount Gerizim when she said to Jesus, 'Our fathers worshipped on this mountain, and you Jews say that in Jerusalem is the place where one ought to worship' (John 4:20). Self-righteous Samaritans would not come as sinners to Mount Ebal, the place of the curse, but they built their altar on Mount Gerizim, with its hoped-for blessings. So Jesus had to say to her, 'You worship what you do not know' (v. 22). Today, the self-righteous Samaritans among us—and there are many—will not come as sinners, confessing their guilt and sin, to the substitutionary sacrifice on Mount Calvary (the place of the curse), but they go as righteous people seeking blessing at the altar of their own making. They go, as it were, to Mount Gerizim, hoping for blessing, and they 'worship what they do not know'.

Churches have many self-righteous, nominal Christians, who presume that they have blessing without ever having gone personally to Calvary. They are good people, sincere people, lovely people—but they have never known the relief of sins forgiven and the joy of the indwelling life of Christ. They presume that they are true Christian men and women when really they have merely accepted mentally the truths of the gospel and know nothing of the mighty regenerating change which the incoming life of Christ brings. They know nothing of the wonder and thrill of feasting on the slain but risen Lamb. They worship 'what they do not know'. You cannot bypass Calvary. The way of the cross leads home; there is no other way but this. Calvary is the starting point—always.

THE PARTICIPATION—THE CURSES AND THE BLESSINGS

In Deuteronomy 27–28 we see the instructions as to how this part of the ceremony was to be conducted. Six tribes were to stand on Mount Ebal and six tribes on Mount Gerizim. Joshua was to call out all the curses and the people would say 'Amen' to each one. He would then call out all the blessings and all the people would say 'Amen' to each one. Joshua's voice rang loud and clear in that wonderful amphitheatre. The 'Amen's thundered forth from thousands of throats as the people affirmed the righteous laws of God to whom they were now committing themselves.

THE NECESSITY OF THE WORD OF GOD

It was written for all to see

Great stones were plastered with lime or gypsum and the law of God was written on the plaster on those stones. The words were to be written 'very plainly', for all to see (Deuteronomy 27:8). Note that they were written in the common language of the people so that all could read it. God wants men and women to read and understand what he has written and what he requires. Translation is essential. The correct understanding of the Word of God and its application to our lives keeps us in God's way and leads us aright.

Because of the time factor it is probable that only the salient features of the law were written. The law of God would remain a standing protest against the sins of the people of the land and would rebuke the Israelites should they stray from God.

It was read for all to hear

'There was not a word of all that Moses had commanded which Joshua did not read before all the assembly of Israel, with the women, the little ones, and the strangers who were living among them' (v. 35). Some prefer to hear only the blessings and the acceptable parts of the Bible, but Joshua read both the blessings and the curses. It was all there. Paul said, 'For I have not shunned to declare to you the whole counsel of God' (Acts 20:27), blessings and curses, heaven and hell.

The centrality of the Word

This was a tremendous occasion, for the ark of God, the sacred emblem of the presence of the Lord, had been brought, and all Israel with their elders, officers and judges stood on either side of the ark before the priests and Levites. The ark was central to the proceedings. God was in the midst of his people. What a sight to see the nation assembled on and between these two mountains! What an epoch-making moment! It included 'the women, the little ones, and the strangers' (v. 35). All were involved in the declaration and acceptance of the Word of God. The children were not separated to play games while the Word was read. It brings home the necessity of having everybody in the worship service, and of the worth and solemnity of the reading of the Word. The Word dominated the scene and had complete authority over the whole nation. They were now more than ever before the people of the Book. They were all worshipping God and committing their lives to him.

The instruction of the Word

In the worship of God here at Shechem emphasis was given to the Word of God. The Word of God should always be prominent, lest worship become distorted or perverted. The Word of God keeps us from error, meaningless repetition and undetected deviation. We are kept safe from wild eccentricities on the one hand and meaningless rites and dead ritual on the other. We are to continue in the biblical pattern of God-appointed worship.

Worship must include not only the sacraments of Gilgal (the Passover and circumcision), but also the instructions of Shechem. We worship in spirit (earnestly) and in truth (intelligently). Our minds are engaged and opened to God's law. The nation of Israel was now committed to God and to his law. It was a great day in Israel!

As we give ourselves to God and to his Word, and keep his commandments, the curses from Mount Ebal will cease to condemn us and Mount Gerizim will rain its blessings upon us.

May it ever be so! Amen and Amen!

Failure with the Gibeonites (9:1–27)

The kings of the land had formed a formidable coalition against their common enemy—Israel. They had all heard of the extermination of the inhabitants of the conquered cities. They fearfully assumed that, unless they did something about it, that would be their fate, too, so they formed a league to oppose the people of God. They sank whatever differences they might have had and pooled their resources to attack Israel.

This is a picture of the enemy's reaction. In the great ceremony of dedication at Mounts Gerizim and Ebal, the people of Israel had only just affirmed their allegiance to the Word of God and committed themselves wholeheartedly to him when the opposition began. Whenever a Christian experiences special blessing he or she is on the verge of another full-scale assault by the devil.

The chapter begins with: 'And [when the kings] heard about it … they gathered together to fight with Joshua and Israel with one accord' (vv. 1–2). The blessing of crossing the Jordan was followed by huge battles. We are not ignorant of Satan's devices and must watch for his attacks whenever God is pleased to bless. Has he blessed you? Get on your knees and plead his protection, for sooner or later you will feel the attack of the enemy and you don't know where it will come from.

The deceit

Gibeon came with guile and caught the Israelites off guard. Israel never expected such a confrontation. Gibeon acted with great deceit to secure peace and to save their skins. Gibeon lay about twelve kilometres (eight miles) north and slightly west of Jerusalem, so they were very close neighbours to Israel. In fact, they were Hivites (v. 7) from four cities in that area—Gibeon, Chephirah, Beeroth and Kirjath Jearim (v. 17). Gibeon was a 'great city ... greater than Ai, and all its men were mighty' (10:2), but they 'worked craftily' (9:4) and deceived Israel by their clever methods. They 'took old sacks on their donkeys [and] old wineskins torn and mended' (v. 4), and came to Israel, pretending to be people who had been on a long journey from a far country.

They came to Gilgal of all places (v. 6), the camp of Israel, where the people had committed themselves to God in the Passover and by circumcision—to Gilgal they came in their daring deception. Their bread was mouldy and their clothes and shoes had apparently become old and worn because of the long journey—evidence indeed should anyone doubt their story. They had heard of the fame of Israel and wanted to make an alliance with her.

They did not speak of Jericho or Ai, for that would have betrayed their position, as these battles had only recently taken place, and they came from a far country! They did not speak of the country from which they came. Naming it would be too risky, so they chose to evade the issue. They intentionally omitted information in order to keep up their deceitful front.

Sometimes it is not what people say that betrays them—it is what they do not say. Apostate preachers will speak smoothly about many good things in the gospel but they will leave other basic issues unsaid, and the gullible will not discern the difference. The preachers will be accepted on the harmless issues they present and will lead the people on to a powerless gospel with no message. The people are deceived and the church desperately weakened.

The Gibeonites spoke of what God had done for Israel in Egypt forty years before, and what he did to the two kings of the Amorites east of Jordan (vv. 9–10). The deeds of the God of Israel formed the basis of their coming to make an alliance with the people of such a God: '... your servants have come, because of the name of the LORD your God' (v. 9). Having heard of his fame they wanted to meet the people who served such a wonderful God. They were wily in their dress and mouldy provisions, and wily in their speech. They lied about their country; they lied about their provisions; they lied about their clothes; they lied about their consecration; they lied about their intentions of being servants.

They spoke so appreciatively of Israel's God, and, of course, of the people who served such a God, that Joshua and the men of Israel smelt a rat: 'Perhaps you dwell among us; so how can we make a covenant with you?' they asked. 'We are your servants', was the Gibeonites' soft reply (vv. 7–8), but their words were deceitful, for they hoped for an alliance in terms of something like equality—'Make a covenant with us,' they said (v. 6). And it was to be immediate! '*Now* therefore, make a covenant with us' (v. 11). They did not want any delays lest their fraud be discovered.

Without looking to God for guidance, Joshua and the rulers of Israel made a covenant with them, allowing them to live. They secured a treaty of peace and saved their lives! No swords! No spears! Just deceit. Israel never dreamed that opposition would come in this way, and they were deceived by the trickery and guile of the enemy. How could they be so gullible? Satan comes not only as a roaring lion (1 Peter 5:8), but also as a subtle serpent (Genesis 3:1). Full-frontal attacks there are, yes, but there is also a wiliness that would try to outmanoeuvre us. The deceit of Judas in the camp is much more difficult to deal with than the open opposition of Caiaphas. The hiss of the serpent is to be feared more than the roar of the lion. 'We are not ignorant of his [Satan's] devices,' said Paul (2 Corinthians 2:11). Jesus said, 'Watch and pray' (Mark 13:33). For the first time in the record of God's people there stood this day on holy ground in the camp at Gilgal a company of people who were indeed Israel's enemies. The Israelites, set apart for God, were now mingled with those whom God had commanded them to destroy.

Alas, the Gibeonites of today have crept into the church, into personal Christian lives, into the Christian's business life, into active church work!

They are weakening the church on every hand, and sapping away at the very heart of the church. In business, how easy it is to cut a few corners here and there to make more profit! In married life, how many think that they can get away with moral deception!

How easily we can be deceived by outward appearances! Samuel judged from outward appearance and thought that Eliab, Jesse's eldest son, was to be king in Saul's stead; but God said, 'Man looks at the outward appearance, but the LORD looks at the heart' (1 Samuel 16:7). Paul condemned 'those who boast in appearance and not in heart' (2 Corinthians 5:12). Satan often dresses up evil as good. He has 'false apostles, deceitful workers, transforming themselves into apostles of Christ' (2 Corinthians 11:13). Satan himself 'transforms himself into an angel of light' (2 Corinthians 11:14). The Gibeonites looked as if they were good people from a far country and they deceived the leaders of Israel into making a treaty with them.

DECEIVED FROM WITHIN

'There's nothing harmful in this,' say the deceivers; but should we respond to the temptation we destroy our distinctive testimony and heavenly character. We forge a friendly alliance and lose our clear witness. It weakens our reason, impairs the tenderness of our conscience and obscures our sense of God. We are among the worldlings, and their laughter drowns the Spirit's voice and chokes the springs of praise. God's presence is stolen from our hearts and prayer loses its power. All unaware, we have been deceived. The unholy alliance was not promptly refused and we have been wooed away into a downward spiritual spiral. The modern-day Gibeonites have done their work of deception and succeeded in weakening our testimony.

DECEIVED FROM WITHOUT

There are those who want to join the Christian fellowship yet who are far from grace. Should the church officers be deceived and the persons whom they have accepted be likeable and strong, yet not truly born again, it could well be a recipe for disaster down the line when issues are considered which need a biblical stance. Those who do not know God will not take the biblical position but will rely on human reason. If they have a following, the church could well be split. The Gibeonites have again deceived and broken up the fellowship.

DECEIVED FROM WITHIN OUR OWN HEARTS

'The heart is deceitful above all things, and desperately wicked; who can know it?' (Jeremiah 17:9). A Christian could easily persuade him- or herself that natural self-will is a holy zeal for God, or that impatience is really spiritual earnestness, or that laziness is careful caution. We can be deluded by 'the deceitfulness of sin' (Hebrews 3:13). We can be deceived by the Gibeonites within our own breasts. Pride is deeply lodged and we may assume that we are more spiritual than we are. 'Do not be haughty, but fear' (Romans 11:20). May the Lord free us from the intrigues of fallen flesh. Only he can cleanse the heart and purify the motives.

The failure to discern

THEIR UNEASY HESITATION

The men of Israel said, 'Perhaps you dwell among us; so how can we make a covenant with you?' (v. 7). Joshua said, 'Who are you, and where do you come from?' (v. 8). There was unease; there were doubts; Joshua and the men of Israel were not convinced.

Unfortunately they did not pursue their questions and neither did they get satisfactory answers. They had listened to the plausible words and accepted their deceit.

Doubts about important issues could be placed in our minds by the Holy Spirit, and it is always good to test these well before committing ourselves to a course of action which could have far-reaching consequences. Take care that you have the peace of God ruling in your heart before taking the course set before you.

THEIR INADEQUATE PERCEPTION

The Gibeonites 'pretended to be ambassadors' (v. 4). Real ambassadors would be careful to be well dressed and presentable before foreign dignitaries in order to impress, but these Gibeonites came with old clothes and mouldy bread. If they were true representatives they would try to bring good things from their country in order to gain a position from which they could strike a favourable treaty. If only the men of Israel had taken a little time to consider these issues, they would have seen the deceit. 'Beloved, do not believe every spirit, but test the spirits, whether they are of God' (1 John 4:1).

THEIR LACK OF PRAYER

The people were faced with this Gibeonite plot, yet we read the fatal words: 'The men of Israel ... did not ask counsel of the LORD' (v. 14). This was the crux of the whole matter! Israel failed to seek God. They relied on their own judgement. They acted naturally, not spiritually.

Joshua had done this once before, after the victory of Jericho and in the matter of Ai, when he badly miscalculated, and now he does it again! He is again found wanting immediately after reading the law to the people of Israel at Mounts Ebal and Gerizim. That mighty moment preceded the failure with the Gibeonites. Again we see that Satan attacks straight after blessing. Let us take Jesus' word to heart: 'Watch!'

'Trust in the LORD with all your heart, and lean not on your own understanding; in all your ways acknowledge him, and he shall direct your paths' (Prov. 3:5–6). Lean not on your own understanding! Our understanding could well be an unsafe guide. The way that seems so right might not be God's way. If in doubt, allow time to pass while you hold the matter before the Lord. Trust him to banish confusion and to bring his peace to your heart. When there is a hurried, insistent compulsion, the constraint is almost certainly not of God. Don't allow yourself to be rushed into taking decisions. Never decide an important issue under strong feelings. Wait on God. The peace of God is unquestionably the umpire of the soul.

The outcome

THE DISCOVERY (VV. 16–17)

It took three days for the truth to emerge—then the Gibeonites were exposed. The Israelites came upon their cities, all just north of Jerusalem. The deceptions of sin were discovered, but they had now made a league with the deceivers and would have to live with that treaty for the rest of their lives. If we yield to deception and forge an unalterable treaty, we may well have to live with the consequences for the rest of our lives. We may have to eat the fruits of our folly.

THE DISSATISFACTION (V. 18)

Obedient to their treaty, the rulers prevented the people from putting the Gibeonites to the sword. They honoured that which they had pledged before God, but the whole assembly grumbled against the rulers who had swallowed the lie and made the treaty. They would be held accountable before God for not carrying out his commands to destroy the Gibeonites, and they would be deprived of much spoil and land which would have been theirs had they done what God wanted them to do. They felt hard done by—they were not happy!

THE DEFENCE (VV. 19–20)

The Gibeonites were spared when they were under the sentence of death. Their salvation was undeserved—mercy prevailed. They were spared because of the oath which was made in the name of 'the Lord God of Israel' (v. 19). The name of the Lord was their salvation. That Name would not be violated. The oath would be upheld.

So it is with those who are outside of grace—they may be saved undeservedly by the Name of the Lord.

THE DECISION (VV. 21–27)

The confrontation (v. 22)

Joshua confronted them head-on. He went for the jugular: 'Why have you deceived us?' Sin was exposed as sin, and called by that name. Many are too afraid to speak straight on the question of sin. No! Sin must be confronted as sin so that repentance and restoration can result. If this is not done, the cancer simply stays and grows.

The curse (v .23)

'Now therefore, you are cursed, and none of you shall be freed from being slaves.' Sin brings a curse. Be not deceived: sin will not enrich your character or bless your life. Sin spoils your life here on earth and cancels the possibility of eternal life in heaven. You cannot escape the results of engaging with this defiling thing called sin.

Their case (v. 24)

They carefully rehearsed their case before Joshua: 'Your servants were clearly told that the LORD your God commanded his servant Moses to give you all the land, and to destroy all the inhabitants of the land from before you; therefore we were very much afraid for our lives because of you, and have done this thing.' They *heard* the word, they *believed* it and they *misused* it. 'Because [of what we heard] *therefore* ... [we] have done this thing.' They blamed the word for their deceit—they blamed God! The Word is used to justify all kinds of sin and God is a convenient excuse.

Their committal (v. 25)

'Do with us as it seems good and right to do to us.' They were so glad to have their lives spared that they did not object to the sentence imposed upon them. They readily submitted themselves to Joshua's judgement. So sinners come to Christ, rejoicing in their deliverance from judgement, submitting themselves unreservedly to him and ready to do his bidding.

Their charge (vv. 26–27)

'And that day Joshua made them woodcutters and water carriers for the congregation and for the altar of the LORD ... even to this day.' They were to be manual servants to Israel. Even from the mistakes which had been made, good might come. They would be servants at the altar and would aid Israel in her service to God. Even if you have unfortunately entered into an alliance with a Gibeonite, God can still bring good from the situation. All is not lost.

The Israelites who had been wronged by this treaty were *recompensed*, for they were provided with much-needed good servants.

This treaty *restricted evil*, for the Gibeonites were now to serve at the altar and not go a-whoring after their own gods. The likelihood of their corrupting Israel by introducing their gods was virtually cancelled, for at the altar they would be taught to serve the true God. The descendants of these Gibeonites were the Nethinim, who held a place of honour in the temple centuries later (1 Chr. 9:2; Ezra 8:20). The grace of God turned even this drastic error around and those who had been enemies of God had now become his servants. How great is the grace of our wonderful God!

Rescuing Gibeon, and the southern campaigns (10:1–43)

Chapter 10 divides neatly into:

- the battle at Gibeon (vv. 1–14);
- the episode of the five kings (vv. 16–27);
- brief reports of victories in the south (vv. 28–39);
- a summary of the southern conquests (vv. 40–42).

In this chapter we see the great and decisive battle that brings in the succession of victories and the subjugation of the land. This was the biggest fight which Joshua had yet fought. Joshua penetrated Canaan through the centre and split the Canaanite powers so that he could not be attacked by the whole land at once; this battle at Gibeon was the one that determined the success of this plan and the future course of events. Joshua then turned southwards and conquered 'from Kadesh Barnea as far as Gaza, and all the country of Goshen, even as far as Gibeon' (v. 41). His skilled strategy worked.

The attack by the Amorites (vv. 1–5)

Finding that Gibeon had made terms with Israel, Adoni-Zedek, the king of Jerusalem, summoned the king of Hebron and neighbouring kings to go up with him against Gibeon. He was unwilling to attempt to make peace with Israel and he was determined that none of his near neighbours would do so either. In his persuasion of them to follow his policy we see how a strong character can lead others to do evil. Israel had previously dealt with separate cities, Jericho and Ai, but now five Amorite kings joined forces, namely, the kings of Jerusalem, Hebron, Jarmuth, Lachish and Eglon.

Notice that they were all neighbours of Gibeon—fellow Canaanites. Opposition sometimes comes from those who are close to you. At this point these coalition forces were out of their walled cities which would have taken so long to subdue by siege. They were out in the open on the battlefield, attempting to punish the turncoat Gibeonites and making it possible for Joshua to engage in battle with them.

These kings regarded Gibeon as a traitor city; its defection aroused the fiercest animosity among its neighbouring cities. Gibeon was a formidable frontier city and for these people tamely to yield to Israel alarmed Adoni-Zedek, king of Jerusalem, who was only a few kilometres away. He had lost what he had counted upon as being a powerful ally. Other cities might follow suit and they might all be conquered and exterminated like Jericho and Ai! He feared for his life and was incensed against the Gibeonites. By overwhelming and occupying Gibeon they might be able to hinder the onward march of the conquering Israelites.

Suddenly, the men of Gibeon found themselves confronted by vast hordes of infuriated warriors who were eager to wreak vengeance on those who dared to make a league with Israel. Adoni-Zedek would crush the Gibeonites while Joshua and his men were away at Gilgal, and would make an object lesson of Gibeon in case others were tempted to follow their example. In the battle with evil forces, Satan may try to intimidate us by a great show of force. Let us take courage, for 'if God is for us, who can be against us?' (Romans 8:31).

The intervention by Joshua (vv. 6–10)
THE APPEAL FROM GIBEON (V. 6)

The Gibeonites did not rely on the strength of their city walls or on the prowess, skill and valour of their mighty men (v. 2). Instead, they sent immediately to Joshua for help. Their strength lay outside of themselves in the one to whom they had committed their lives and who had sworn with an oath to save them from death.

It was a humble appeal

They said, 'Do not forsake your servants.' Such language breathed a spirit of dependence. They realized that they had no strength to repulse the enemy. We too have no strength against the enemy. Only God is sufficient to deal with Satan's attacks. It is in our conscious weakness that our strength lies. When we come to God in prayer we come in humility—there is no other way to come.

It was a direct appeal

They appealed directly to Joshua. In time of trouble we go to our mighty ruler, Jesus Christ.

This ruler was able and powerful. Our blessed Master is able and powerful. Jordan and Jericho are but pictures of his mighty conquest at Calvary, when he scattered the forces of evil.

They would expect Joshua to be loyal to the treaty. Jesus cares for us more than anyone else in the world and he will keep his word: '[Cast] all your care upon him, for he cares for you' (1 Peter 5:7).

It was an urgent appeal

'Do not forsake your servants; come up to us quickly, save us and help us, for all the kings of the Amorites who dwell in the mountains have gathered together against us.' They unburdened their hearts and explained their hopeless position. Without Joshua's intervention they were doomed. They had no hope before this formidable coalition. They needed immediate salvation—'come up to us quickly'. The situation was urgent!

The only way in which lost souls can find deliverance and salvation is for them to recognize that they have no strength whatever to save themselves. They have to cry to the only One who can save them from their sin and God's righteous judgement. He is able to save them if only they would call on him!

When it seems that you are about to be overwhelmed by the forces of evil, cry mightily to God! He is the only One who is able to deliver in every trial. The psalmist cried, 'Make haste to help me, O Lord, my salvation!' (Psalm 38:22).

THE ACTION BY JOSHUA (VV. 7–10)

There was alacrity

Joshua responded immediately. He did not sit around wondering what he ought to do, but acted with speed and determination. This is typical of Joshua, for when he saw something to be done he did it with his might. What an example!

There was sympathy

In the Gospels we find that Jesus never failed to answer an appeal for help. He was available to rich Zacchaeus, to poor blind Bartimaeus, to the Jew, Samaritan and Gentile. He never turned a deaf ear to any cry of distress. And here Joshua is a beautiful picture of our beloved Lord. He responded quickly to the cry for help. We can call upon God with confidence, knowing that he will hear us and come to our aid.

There was integrity

Joshua and the Israelites kept their word. They would not dishonour God by breaking their agreement with the Gibeonites. The honour of God was at stake and they were true to their word, even though Gibeon had been so deceitful.

There was dependency

Joshua was now going in the strength of the Lord, for God said to him, 'Do not fear them, for I have delivered them into your hand; not a man of them shall stand before you' (v. 8). Going into the biggest battle of his career, he needed the encouragement of God—and he got it. 'Do not fear,' God said, 'I have delivered them into your hand.' What more could he ask for than that! Conscious of divine companionship and strength, he took up arms. His confidence was now not in himself, but in the God who was leading him to the victory.

There was agility

They 'ascended from Gilgal' (v. 7). The mighty coalition held the high ground with great advantage and Joshua and his men had to ascend from around 240 metres below sea level to about 450 metres above sea level (around 700 metres in total) in the distance of about twenty-five kilometres (fifteen miles).

This was an arduous, demanding and hazardous mountain climb. Even though God had said that the victory was theirs they did not use this assurance as an excuse for slackness. There was self-sacrificing effort. Divine help does not exclude human exertion. They set off immediately and climbed through the night.

They acted sacrificially

Sleep was sacrificed; comforts were denied. To help the Gibeonites the Israelites had to expend great effort. If we want to accomplish anything for the Lord then we will have to give ourselves determinedly and wholeheartedly to his work. Nothing can replace hard work, and that often means the sacrifice of time, energy and means. Only thus will the gospel chariot roll!

There was strategy

'Joshua therefore came upon them suddenly, having marched all night from Gilgal' (v. 9). Joshua's skill as a military leader is now clearly seen. Under the cover of darkness they would strike unexpectedly. This was a sudden, surprise attack which threw the armies into confusion. Joshua took the opportunity when it knocked. Opportunity doesn't knock for long! Recognize it! Seize it! Use your opportunities well!

There was victory

'So the LORD routed them before Israel, killed them with a great slaughter at Gibeon, chased them along the road that goes to Beth Horon, and struck them down as far as Azekah and Makkedah' (v. 10). This was a crucial battle, for if Joshua had failed here, the Canaanites would have descended upon Gilgal and destroyed Israel. This was the first time that the Canaanites were out of their fortified cities and on open ground. God used the mistake made with the Gibeonites to accelerate the conquest of the land. God can turn our blunders to good effect to accomplish his purposes. The Scripture says that *God* routed the enemy. It was realized that the Israelites' skills and abilities came from God. We are what we are because we have received it all from him, and any victories we might gain are his victories. We cannot take the credit; he must get all the glory.

The intervention by God (vv. 11–15)

Because 'the LORD fought for Israel' (v. 14), there was a remarkable victory. This was in fact *the* decisive battle in the conquest of Canaan—and God stepped in! There were two mighty miracles: the hailstones and the sun standing still. At the heart of it all we read, 'Then Joshua spoke to the LORD' (v. 12). Joshua prayed! He was in touch with God in the midst of the battle! What happened?

Joshua had approached from the east and in all probability controlled the road south to Jerusalem, for the defeated coalition soldiers did not return that way. They were thoroughly defeated and fled panic-stricken at breakneck speed before Israel westward from the mountain heights down the slopes to Azekah and Makkedah, Makkedah being about twenty-four kilometres (fifteen miles) away from Gibeon, halfway to the Mediterranean sea. 'If only night would fall and hide us from the wrath of Israel.'

THE HAILSTONES

In the midst of this desperate flight God fought for Israel. 'The LORD cast down large hailstones from heaven on them ... There were more who died from the hailstones than the children of Israel killed with the sword' (v. 11). Notice, firstly, the size of the hailstones: they were 'large', capable of killing a man. Chunks of ice crashed down on the fleeing multitudes. Secondly, these hailstones descended with mighty force, killing men outright. God's judgement is sure and can be swift, too. Thirdly, they were accurately directed to the enemy alone. The whole artillery of heaven suddenly opened fire. Even though the Israelites were in close contact with the Canaanites, none of the deadly missiles fell on them, but for the Canaanites there was no escaping God's wrath. God trained his ammunition with accuracy on the enemy. The cry of the vanquished, the shout of the pursuer and the clatter of the hailstones filled the air. God intervened and gave the victory. This was seen by both Israel and the enemy alike.

THE LONG DAY

Joshua said, '"Sun, stand still over Gibeon, and Moon, in the Valley of Aijalon." ... So the sun stood still' (vv. 12–13). Joshua wanted victory before night fell, so he exercised his full confidence in a miracle-working God. His faith in God exceeded his understanding of nature, and he claimed that God would do the impossible to help his people. What an amazing prayer! And he prayed it 'in the sight of Israel' (v. 12). This was a public exhibition of faith. Pretty risky! At the end of the account of the day we read, 'And there has been no day like that, before it or after it, that the LORD heeded the voice of a man' (v. 14). What power there is in believing prayer! 'If you ask anything in my name, I will do it,' said Jesus (John 14:14). Joshua doubtless had an extraordinary impression upon his spirit, which he knew to be of God, in order to be able to pray such a prayer. God wished to accomplish his purpose, which required that man be part of that purpose by asking that he reveal his power in this specific way.

It was also an expression of Joshua's utter dedication to the work of

God, for when he could have had some respite after fighting all day, he denied himself that opportunity and desperately wanted the job done by the lengthening of the day. 'Zeal for your house has eaten me up' (Psalm 69:9).

Sceptics have made a meal of this long day. They have poured scorn upon the whole incident, but it all depends on how big your God is! God controlled the gradual descent of the sun. God upholds and governs all things in heaven and on earth, and he who created the universe would have no trouble in temporarily adjusting the speed the earth turns on its axis. To believe that this happened is not an insult to intelligence but a revelation of the power of an omnipotent God.

At the end of this remarkable day, Joshua, and all Israel with him, returned to the camp at Gilgal (v. 15). The greatest battle for the conquest of Canaan had been fought and decisively won.

The treatment of the five kings (vv. 16–27)

Mopping-up operations were in progress and while Israel was 'slaying them with a very great slaughter' (v. 20), Joshua was informed that the five kings had been found hidden in a cave in Makkedah. That was a fortunate and very significant find!

THEIR INCARCERATION

Joshua's response was that they should continue pursuing their enemies but that they place large stones against the mouth of the cave, imprisoning the kings in the place which they had thought to be a refuge. He concluded the battle before punishing the kings. He had the enemy on the run and would not be sidetracked. Had he not pursued and destroyed the enemy, many would have taken refuge in the fortified cities and would have given huge problems in the future. His priorities were always focused. How necessary to have our priorities right and to stick by them!

After the fighting had subsided, and when a few had escaped to the fortified towns, the people gathered to Joshua at Makkedah. It was a mighty victory, for 'no one moved his tongue against any of the children of Israel' (v. 21). The fear of God had fallen upon the land and they were awed to silence.

The cave was opened and the five kings were brought out: kings of Jerusalem, Hebron, Jarmuth, Lachish and Eglon. Only a few hours before, they had proudly stood at the head of their armies, but then they had seen them almost completely annihilated by the sword of Israel and by the artillery of heaven. Rather than trying to rally their forces, they fled for their lives and hid in a cave twenty-five kilometres (fifteen miles) away from the battle site at Gibeon. They supposedly thought that the darkness would hide their retreat from the cave to their own fortified cities, but they were seen. Had not God said, 'I have delivered them into your hand' (v. 8)? Joshua now had no choice in the matter of their punishment, for God had said, 'You shall conquer them and utterly destroy them' (Deuteronomy 7:2).

THEIR HUMILIATION

Joshua now held a solemn court-martial. The kings were brought before him. It was the moment of their humiliation. They stood defeated, discovered and exposed. For them there would be no mercy. Joshua 'said to the captains of the men of war who went with him, "Come near, put your feet on the necks of these kings." And they ... put their feet on their necks' (v. 24). This put the conquered in a place of great dishonour. It was an acted parable and an assuring sign to God's people that from now on their enemies would be under them. It was a point of deepest infamy and heaviest vengeance for the kings. While they grovelled with their faces in the dust, Joshua delivered a word of great encouragement to the leaders who trampled on their necks: 'Do not be afraid, nor be dismayed,' he said. 'Be strong and of good courage, for thus the LORD will do to all your enemies against whom you fight' (v. 25). Joshua was breathing confidence into their hearts.

Joshua emphasized that it was God who had won the battle for them. They would not be able to boast of their achievements, for God had fought for Israel and had given them the victory.

THEIR EXECUTION

Being hanged publicly on a tree brings great despising. Their soldiers were cut down by the sword and slain by the hailstones, but the humiliation for the leaders extended to the feet-on-neck episode and beyond. They were struck and killed, and then hanged on trees (v. 26). What a despicable ending! 'He who is hanged is accursed of God' (Deuteronomy 21:23). The curse of God rested upon them for their evil lives and for opposing the plans and purposes of God.

Joshua was nevertheless careful to obey God's laws. He cut them down from the tree at the time of the going down of the sun (v. 27), for God had also said, 'His body shall not remain overnight on the tree' (Deuteronomy 21:23).

THEIR COMMEMORATION

'They … cast them into the cave where they had been hidden, and laid large stones against the cave's mouth, which remain until this very day' (v. 27). This was the fifth cairn, or heap of stones, which had been raised in the land of Canaan. It commemorated another instructive event. The first two cairns commemorated the crossing of Jordan. The third was raised over Achan to remind them that sin does not pay. The fourth was raised over the king of Ai's body to commemorate a great victory, and this, the fifth, reminded them of God's holiness, justice and help to his own.

The central and southern campaigns (vv. 28–42)

Joshua was on a roll! The conquest in this great battle put fear into the hearts of everyone in the land. The Canaanites knew of Jericho, of Ai, and now this ignominious defeat of the united forces of the five kings! They quaked in their sandals before the ongoing rush of the conquering Israelites.

Joshua could have taken time off and rested for a while, but he had to finish the task. What had at first begun as a single battle was expanded into a mighty campaign which encompassed the central and southern areas of Canaan. Joshua capitalized on the victory and plunged into the heart of the enemy, conquering one city after another.

Notice that the army's efforts were constant. They did not slacken, but continued till all the great battles had been fought and the task was complete. Their efforts were also combined. They were united in their efforts. All the Israelites were committed to the task. No complaints are recorded. They worked together until the job was done. United, dedicated, helpful co-operation will win the day. May God give us just that.

Makkedah was taken that day and 'He utterly destroyed them—all the people who were in it' (v. 28). Next was Libnah, and Joshua 'struck it and all the people who were in it with the edge of the sword' (v. 30). Then followed the formidable fortress of Lachish, which he conquered 'the second day' (v. 32). Sennacherib, king of Assyria, failed to take Lachish (2 Kings 19:7–8), and Lachish was one of the last two cities to be conquered when Nebuchadnezzar invaded the land (Jeremiah 34:7). Some things in our lives are more difficult to conquer than others, but that must not deter us from making further efforts to do so. Next on the list was Eglon, and 'all the people who were in it he utterly destroyed that day' (v. 35). Then Joshua went to Hebron, way down south. They 'struck it with the edge of the sword—its king, all its cities, and all the people who were in it; he left none remaining' (v. 37). He moved further south to Debir and 'utterly destroyed all the people who were in it' (v. 39). 'So Joshua conquered all the land: the mountain country and the South and the lowland and the wilderness slopes, and all their kings; he left none remaining' (v. 40). He conquered Kadesh Barnea in the extreme south and Gaza near the coast (v.

41). All these victories were attained 'because the LORD God of Israel fought for Israel' (v. 42).

The home base at Gilgal (v. 43)

The land was subdued, and after all these mighty conquests 'Joshua returned, and all Israel with him, to the camp at Gilgal.' This was their home base. Great to have a home base—for rest and comfort after the battles of life! Every kind of warfare takes its toll. They had just been through a period of extreme exertion and exhaustion, and with relief and gratitude they were able to return to Gilgal, their place of rest and healing.

Do you have a Gilgal to which you can return? A place where you can be alone with God and experience his healing presence and strengthening hand? A place of intimate communion with God? Do you?

Gilgal is also a place where we can be strengthened by one another's company, fellowship and spiritual conversations; where we can share with one another about the things of God and are encouraged day by day. Gilgal—blessed retreat!

The question of ethics

The ethics of this wholesale slaughter have, of course, been questioned, but this issue should be understood in the light of three things: the command of God, the wickedness of the Canaanites and the degeneracy and contagion of sin.

THE COMMAND OF GOD

'But of the cities of these peoples which the LORD your God gives you as an inheritance, you shall let nothing that breathes remain alive' (Deuteronomy 20:16). Joshua fulfilled the commandment of the Lord and destroyed the populace.

This is surely a picture of our own lives, for we are commanded to get rid of every sin. We cannot tolerate any evil in our lives. We dare not leave sin lurking in the hidden recesses of our hearts. Pride, a desire for self-glorification and unconquered lust ruin our witness and make our lives miserable. We wistfully wonder when, if ever, we shall be victorious. Christ can and will cleanse our sin; we can be transformed by divine grace from being weak and ineffective Christians to those who are vibrant, pure and God-glorifying. There is power in the blood of Christ to cleanse from every sin.

THE WICKEDNESS OF THE CANAANITES
The cup of their iniquity was overflowing. If this were allowed to continue, the land would never be cleared of its evil practices. Judgement was at the door and they were to be the recipients of divine wrath.

THE CONTAGION OF SIN
Evil is contagious. God had said that the Canaanites should be destroyed 'lest they teach you to do according to all their abominations which they have done for their gods, and you sin against the LORD your God' (Deuteronomy 20:18). If we don't destroy the 'Canaanites', they could destroy us. The call to separation is clear in the Word of God, and it is for us to obey, renounce every form of sin and worldliness, and turn with all our hearts to the Lord.

The conquest of northern Canaan (11:1–23)

Chapter 11 mirrors chapter 10, in that there is an alliance of a number of northern cities which fight with the Israelites on the open battlefield (10:1–14; 11:1–9). They are defeated and this is followed by the capture of the cities (10:28–39; 11:10–15), which is followed by a generalizing summary (10:40–42; 11:16–20,23). As in chapter 10, God promises Joshua victory (10:8; 11:6). Joshua obeys the Lord and leads Israel; they also obey and are victorious by using the same tactic: they come upon the Canaanites 'suddenly' (10:9; 11:7).

In verse 18 we read: 'Joshua made war a long time with all those kings.' The long time was about seven years, for when Israel failed at Kadesh Barnea (Deuteronomy 2:14), Caleb was forty years old (Joshua 14:7). From Kadesh Barnea to the crossing of Jordan was thirty-eight years. Caleb was eighty-five years old when the conquest was over (14:10). This means that about seven years had been devoted to the conquest of Canaan.

Having conquered the central and southern sections of the country, Joshua could now turn his attention to the north. If the north were to be conquered, the entire country would be under the control of Israel. It was the north which took the initiative to take up arms and fight against Israel.

The importance of the city

In chapter 10 Adoni-Zedek, king of Jerusalem, was the strong leader of the coalition forces, and in chapter 11 Jabin, king of Hazor, took the lead. 'Hazor was formerly the head of all those kingdoms' (v. 10), so it was natural for Jabin to take the lead and call a number of kings together to the waters of Merom to fight against Israel. The waters of Merom were to the north of the Sea of Galilee, and Hazor was nearby. To this point the northern coalition forces were called and gathered.

Hazor was a massive site that dominated the main branches of the highway leading from Egypt to Mesopotamia and Syria. It was probably the biggest city in Canaan. The three big cities which Joshua had to conquer were Jericho, Jerusalem and Hazor. Gibeon was also a major obstacle with mighty men of war, but it had submitted to the invaders and Jericho and Jerusalem had been vanquished. Hazor now presented a major challenge to Joshua and his forces.

The might of the opposition

Hazor's own interests were now seriously threatened and it was time for them to unite and to mount a concerted attack on Israel. They became the aggressors and therefore Joshua had the right to defend his fledgling nation and punish Hazor with extreme measures. If he did not, they would conquer his army, sweep down on the camp at Gilgal and annihilate the Israelites.

Indignant, and fearful of their own fate, the Canaanites gathered all the forces which they could muster to halt the ruthless advance of these invaders. Jabin called the kings of Madon, Shimron, Achshaph and 'the kings who were from the north, in the mountains, in the plain south of Chinneroth, in the lowland, and in the heights of Dor on the west, to the Canaanites in the east and in the west, the Amorite, the Hittite, the Perizzite, the Jebusite in the mountains, and the Hivite below Hermon' (vv. 2–3). It was a mighty and formidable force—'as many people as the sand that is on the seashore in multitude, with very many horses and chariots' (v. 4). 'Josephus tells us that the allied armies amounted to 300,000 foot, 10,000 horse, and 20,000 chariots of war,' wrote Adam Clarke.[1] They all gathered near to Hazor at the waters of Merom to fight against Israel.

More powers were allied together to fight Israel here than in any other conflict in Canaan. This vast assembly must have been an awesome and terrifying sight. They would doubtless have been assured of an easy victory. They were numerous; they were united; they were trained; they were organized; they were well equipped; they were desperate; they had hard hearts (v. 20). They had the advantages of knowing the terrain, of having their supplies near at hand and of being accustomed to war. The odds were stacked high against Joshua and his army. They had never fought against chariots before. Those fearful chariots with scythes attached to their wheels would tear ruthlessly into the enemy, cutting a bloody swathe of mutilated bodies through the troops, and as they plunged forward the occupants would be able to deliver the artillery which would shatter the forces arrayed against them. There was no hope! This was indeed the greatest battle of Joshua's life.

It is possible today to get a coalition of people against gospel truths and the work of God. The worldlings don't want it; the self-righteous don't want it; the vile sinners don't want it; the atheists don't want it; the humanistic philosophers don't want it. They all join together against the gospel. But the Bible says, 'Though they join forces, the wicked will not go unpunished' (Prov. 11:21). God will have the last word!

In the work of God there are inevitably hard times. Sometimes it would seem that it is just not possible to go on. The pressures are too great; the opposition, coming from such unexpected quarters, is too strong; the hardness of those from whom you had expected such fellowship is too painful; the unfounded criticism is too harsh; the suspicions and snide remarks are too cutting; and the things you hear on the grapevine crush your soul. Don't give up! Don't resign and run away! It's always too soon to quit.

Joshua knew something of what he was up against when he heard of the vast hordes of dedicated soldiers arrayed against him, but he did not give up. God was with him and had given him promises of victory. In the face of such enormous odds he advanced with God at his side and he conquered, for God fought for him. We are on the victory side, and need to realize that God is with us!

The comfort of the promise

God had given Joshua promises before. When he called him to lead Israel, he said 'Do not be afraid, nor be dismayed, for the LORD your God is with you wherever you go' (1:9). When they came to the Jordan, God said, 'As I was with Moses, so I will be with you' (3:7). The crossing was assured because of the word of God to him. When he approached Jericho, God said, 'See! I have given Jericho into your hand' (6:2). After the defeat at Ai, God said to Joshua, 'Do not be afraid, nor be dismayed; take all the people of war with you, and arise, go up to Ai. See, I have given into your hand the king of Ai, his people, his city, and his land' (8:1). When Joshua had to face the southern coalition which was amassed against Gibeon, God said to him, 'Do not fear them, for I have delivered them into your hand' (10:8).

Now he stands before the mightiest alliance of all, and how he needs some assurance from God! Did God forsake him? No! No! God undergirded him with words of comfort and strength: 'Do not be afraid because of them, for tomorrow about this time I will deliver all of them slain before Israel' (11:6). Was Joshua relieved? The forces with which he would soon be engaged would have to deal with the invincible God! He who had given them impossible victories in the past was not going to abandon them now! They would rise from weakness and conquer in God's strength, for he was with them.

When believers are sorely pressed, God whispers, 'He who touches you touches the apple of his eye' (Zechariah 2:8). He says to Joshua, 'Do not be afraid because of them' (v. 6). Those who are arrayed against you will soon themselves be destroyed. 'And the God of peace will crush Satan under your feet shortly' (Romans 16:20). So we can say, 'Behold, God is my salvation, I will trust and not be afraid' (Isaiah 12:2); 'If God is for us, who can be against us?' (Romans 8:31). He gives his children promises which apply to each specific instance—precious and meaningful!

The course of the battle

THE ATTACK WAS SUDDEN

'So Joshua and all the people of war with him came against them suddenly by the waters of Merom, and they attacked them' (v. 7). It was a swift and sudden attack, perhaps at dawn, as before. The Canaanites would have thought that, because of the massive build-up of troops and equipment near Hazor, Joshua would not dare to come anywhere near them but would be cowering in some far-off place, expecting the worst. But Joshua struck 'suddenly'. The enemy rulers did not have a chance to organize their forces. Pandemonium broke out among them, and they fled.

THE BATTLE WAS DIVINELY DIRECTED

Joshua launched his assault based on the promise of his God, who had said, 'Tomorrow ... I will deliver all of them slain before Israel' (v. 6). Tomorrow! That's it! We must attack tomorrow. God's promise did not absolve Joshua of responsibility or activity. He had faith in God to accomplish his purposes, but he was not exempted from total co-operation. Attack he must, and it was to be 'tomorrow'.

The suddenness of the attack was the result of laying hold of God's 'tomorrow'. He dared to rely on what God had said in spite of impossible circumstances, and 'the LORD delivered them into the hand of Israel' (v. 8). Throughout history there have been those who have trusted in God's word to them and have gone on to accomplish great exploits in his Name. The promises were the foundation of everything. If we act upon God's promises, we will see his victory!

GOD'S COMMANDS WERE OBEYED

God gave the instructions and Joshua obeyed. He conquered because he obeyed. Three times we read of his obedience: 'So Joshua did to them as the LORD had told him' (v. 9); 'He utterly destroyed them, as Moses the servant of the LORD had commanded' (v. 12); 'He left nothing undone of all that the

LORD had commanded Moses' (v. 15). It seems that verse 15 is saying, 'Here is a model of God's servant. His chief characteristic is that he obeys God's word.' The conquest narratives from Jericho to Hazor stand as a monument to the great faithfulness of Joshua to the Mosaic law. Often God speaks his will to us through the Scriptures. When we have discerned his will, it is for us to obey and to leave the consequences to him.

THE VICTORY WAS DECISIVE

God's instructions were to kill all the soldiers, to hamstring the horses and to burn the chariots (v. 6). To hamstring is to cut the sinews behind the hooves, rendering the horse useless. Supposedly the Israelites would return later to despatch the horses. This took away much of the enemy's ability to fight, and, with the chariots aflame, they took to their heels. 'Some trust in chariots, and some in horses; but we will remember the name of the LORD our God' (Psalm 20:7). The Israelites would now not be able to use the horses and chariots against the Canaanites and claim that by their cleverness and tactics they had won the victory. God was to have all the glory, and with the horses out of action and the chariots on fire, no one could take the credit for the victory but God.

Israel fell on the enemy and struck them, chasing them towards the north-west to Sidon, westwards to the sea coast (Misrephoth), and into the plain of Mizpah on the east. The rout was complete. The unbelievable had happened. Israel had not merely survived but had conquered, and all because they trusted and obeyed the word of God. The Canaanites had chosen to fight against Israel's God and they had been soundly defeated and destroyed.

For the Christian, Hazor, like Jericho, represents those who stand against the will of God. The kings had schemed and were executing their rebellious plans when God stepped in. God has the last say!

In our own lives, the bigger the difficulties and sins the more impossible it seems for them to be conquered. But even though they stand out like

Hazor as unconquerable foes, when God steps in, it is his battle, and the victory and the glory are his.

THE CITIES WERE TAKEN

'Then he burned Hazor with fire' (v. 11). Archaeologists have been compelled to identify the destruction of Hazor with the Israelite conquest. This was the bitter end of those who opposed God.

'So all the cities of those kings, and all their kings, Joshua took and struck with the edge of the sword. He utterly destroyed them' (v. 12). This follows in rapid succession to Hazor's burning and gives the impression of the speed and effectiveness with which everything was accomplished. Joshua burned no more of the cities, but struck and destroyed all the inhabitants of the 'cities that stood on their mounds' (v. 13). The destruction was complete. 'As the LORD had commanded Moses his servant, so Moses commanded Joshua, and so Joshua did' (v. 15). The spoil of these cities and the livestock were taken as booty by the Israelites.

Just as God used Cyrus to destroy Babylon and to be an instrument of punishment in God's hand (Jeremiah 51:20), so God used Israel to punish the evil inhabitants of Canaan. 'Thus Joshua took all this land' (v. 16).

Joshua swept across the country and conquered in every place. Even the dreaded giant Anakim were conquered, so that 'None of the Anakim were left in the land of the children of Israel; they remained only in Gaza, in Gath, and in Ashdod' (v. 22). It is interesting that the enormous Philistine champion whom David vanquished was 'Goliath, from Gath' (1 Samuel 17:4). He was probably one of the descendants of the Anakim, who were men of great stature. When we don't complete God's will and purpose, later on the results of that disobedience will rise to meet us with stinging acrimony and battles will be once again engaged.

THE LAND WAS SUBDUED

'Joshua gave it as an inheritance to Israel according to their divisions by their tribes' (v.23), yet the tribes had still to drive out the inhabitants of the land. Those who had hidden in caves now emerged and were still in the land. They had to be driven out 'little by little' (Exodus 23:30). It was for the Israelites to claim what was rightfully theirs and drive out those who had been conquered.

So it is with the Christian. God has given us the land of promise. God gives us the riches of heavenly victory through our Lord Jesus Christ. The land has been conquered. The battle has been won. No root of bitterness or shaft of malice may be allowed any place of residence in our hearts to rob us of an abiding communion with him. No! They have no place nor right in our hearts. 'Out! Away! You have no right to be here! You have been conquered and deserve the edge of the sword. Be gone forever! I plead the blood of the cross where you were conquered and defeated.'

Claim the victory! Has Jesus not won it for us on the cross? Has he not 'put away sin by the sacrifice of himself' (Hebrews 9:26)? Claim his mighty victory over all the powers of darkness and hell. Exercise faith! Rest upon his almighty victory over all the evil forces which he has already conquered. No hidden inhabitants attempting to reassert their right to existence should disturb us. We claim the cleansing power of the precious blood of Jesus. Therein is our victory, and we expel by faith those who attempt to contradict their defeat and destruction at Calvary. Claim it now, and trust him to work it out in your life for his praise and glory.

We could summarize this section as follows:

- The area of the conquest (vv. 16–17)—Joshua took all the land.
- The duration of the conquest (v. 18)—as has been pointed out, this was seven years.
- The extent of the conquest (vv. 19–20)—all the cities were taken.
- The special aspect of the conquest (vv. 21–23)—the defeat of the Anakim, the giant race.
- The summary of the conquest—'So Joshua took the whole land' (v. 23).

THE ERRORS OF JOSHUA

Joshua made three strategic blunders. Firstly, he failed to gain control of the coastline and left the western borders in the hands of the Phoenicians in the north and the Philistines in the south. The Gaza strip, the south-west coastline, has given Israel a great deal of trouble down the centuries, and does so even now, almost 3,500 years later. Secondly, he made the disastrous treaty with the Gibeonites. Thirdly, he failed to complete the 'mopping-up' operations. Later we read that the Lord said to Joshua, 'You are old ... and there remains very much land yet to be possessed' (13:1). These errors resulted in grave problems for Israel in the days ahead.

How essential to be diligent to complete all that God sets before us! No lurking carnal elements should be allowed to remain. The 'mopping-up' must be well done. Calvary is where sin has been dealt with, where the victory is proclaimed. To Calvary we must go and find there that he can set us free from those unwholesome issues which spoil our walk with him.

The rest after the conflict

'Then the land rested from war' (v. 23). They had rest! This was rest from the rigours of the wilderness and from the warfare in the land. This to them was indeed God's promised and wonderful rest. 'There remains therefore a rest for the people of God ... Let us therefore be diligent to enter that rest, lest anyone fall according to the same example of disobedience' (Hebrews 4:9,11).

The Sabbath rest for the Christian is a picture of ceasing from labours, just as God did from his (Hebrews 4:10):

Firstly, salvation is not merited by works. We are not saved by works, but through faith (Ephesians 2:8–9). Rest, seen in this way, is the peace of God coming to our hearts when we trust him for salvation.

Secondly, 'rest' could simply be a rest from worry and anxiety. '[Cast] all your care upon him, for he cares for you' (1 Peter 5:7).

Thirdly, it could mean the eternal rest of heaven. This will most certainly be the supreme and final rest for the people of God.

Fourthly, it speaks of Canaan as the land of victory, blessing and rest in the life of a Christian.

Concerning spiritual rest, there is a time when spiritual anxiety ceases when we initially trust the work of the cross; and also (generally some time later, when the struggle to live a holy life in one's own strength ceases and a 'Thanks be to God, who gives us the victory through our Lord Jesus Christ!' rises from the heart), there is an ever-deepening 'rest'. The rest which God gives is the rest of reconciliation, of assured victory, of a surrendered will, of unbroken fellowship, of perfect love and of a heart that perseveres in holiness.

The land of Canaan throughout the whole book of Joshua corresponds in the New Testament to our inheritance in Christ. After his work was finished, Jesus cried out on the cross, 'It is finished!' He had 'put away sin by the sacrifice of himself' (Hebrews 9:26). He had conquered at Calvary and the task was complete. We rest not in a day, but in a Person. Our Sabbath is Jesus, who has taken away our sin, and it is for us to appropriate from him the victory and the rest that he has accomplished and offers to us: 'Take my yoke upon you and learn from me, for I am gentle and lowly in heart, and you will find rest for your souls' (Matthew 11:29). Rest! Ah, rest in the Person who made it all possible. Brethren, we have rest!

This is a rest not of inactivity, of laziness, from weariness after labour, but it is a rest of *satisfaction*. God has accomplished and finished his mighty salvation through the offering of the body of Jesus Christ once for all. It is God's rest! Nothing can be added to the finished work of salvation. Jesus sits in the heavenly places today because he has 'offered one sacrifice for sins forever' (Hebrews 10:12). The demands of God's justice have been satisfied, and for those who trust in him, there is now no condemnation. It is the rest of calm, poise, assurance and satisfaction that the work has been done. That rest is imparted to those who fully trust in the working of his power in their own lives, and who are 'made [to] sit together in the heavenly places in Christ Jesus' (Ephesians 2:6).

God desires that we should enter into his rest in terms of daily experience. The fruit of victory for Christ is rest. We rest in his love, his strength, his purity, his joy, his compassion, his transparency, his zeal, his sacrificial living, his obedience, his commitment and his faithfulness. We are in him, and his life, with all those characteristics in us! This is his rest. These qualities of our blessed Lord fill our hearts as we seek him and desire that he lives his life through us. We share the qualities of his rest in our own hearts as we trust him.

It is such a pity, then, that we exercise so little faith and live as if we had no rest or riches!

Where is the rest which he purchased for us and which he offers to us? Why are we so impatient and irritable, so joyless and moody? Where is the victory then? Ah, this must be appropriated, just as our initial salvation was appropriated. It is by faith that we advance. Remember that the Israelites 'could not enter in because of unbelief' (Hebrews 3:19). The life of faith lives in the promise, in the will, in the power of God. Rest is entered, through death to self in the death of Christ, through faith.

We strain and do our best to live victoriously, but slip back into defeat again. We are trying to get there by our works, but it is not a matter of working but of trusting.

We can do nothing to improve our lot. It is for us to trust in that which has been done—to cease from our own works, our own desperate attempts at self-improvement, and to enter into his rest!

Entering the rest of God is the ceasing from self-effort, and the yielding up oneself in the full surrender of faith to God's working … And how does one rest and cease from his works? It is by ceasing from self. It is only in death that we rest from our works. Jesus entered his rest through death; each one whom he leads into it must pass through death. 'Reckon yourselves to be indeed dead unto sin and alive unto God in Christ Jesus our Lord.' Believe that the death of Christ as an accomplished fact, with all that it means and has effected, is working in you in all its power. You are dead with him and in him. Consent to this and cease from dead works.[2]

Chapter 15

The great missionary Hudson Taylor wrote from China to his sister in England of his spiritual struggles. Here is part of the letter:

Each day brought its register of sin and failure, of lack of power ... Then came the question, 'Is there no rescue?' Must it be thus to the end—constant conflict and instead of victory, too often defeat? I hated my sin, and yet I gained no strength against it ... I thought that holiness, practical holiness, was to be gradually attained by a diligent use of the means of grace. I felt that there was nothing I so much desired in this world, nothing I so much needed. But so far from in any measure attaining it, the more I pursued and strove after it, the more it eluded my grasp, till hope almost died out ... When my agony of soul was at its height, a sentence in a letter from McCarthy was used to open my eyes, and the Spirit of God revealed the truth of our oneness with Jesus as I had never known it before ... I looked to Jesus and I saw (and when I saw, oh, how the joy flowed!) that he had said 'I will never leave you.' Ah, there is rest! I thought. I have striven in vain to rest in him. I'll strive no more ... The sweetest part, if one may speak of one part being sweeter than another, is the rest which full identification with Christ brings.[3]

In the late seventeenth century, Brother Lawrence in France wrote: 'In the noise and clatter of my kitchen while several persons are at the same time calling for different things, I possess God in as great tranquillity as if I were on my knees.'[4] May God give us all that kind of rest and victory!

Notes

1 **Adam Clarke,** *Clarke's Commentary: The Old Testament*, Vol. 2 (New York: Abingdon Press, 1820), p. 53.
2 **Murray,** *The Holiest of All*, pp. 152–153.
3 **J. Hudson Taylor,** quoted in **Colin N. Peckham,** *From Defeat to Victory* (Edinburgh: Faith Mission, 1993), pp. 4–5.
4 **Brother Lawrence,** *The Practice of the Presence of God* (London: Samuel Baxter & Sons, n.d.), p. 43.

Possessing the land: A summary of the conquest (12:1–21:45)

Chapter 12: Kings conquered by Moses and Joshua

Chapter 12 is a record of the conquest of the kings and their cities in Transjordan under Moses (vv. 1–6), and west of the Jordan under Joshua (vv. 7–24).

THE FIRST SECTION (VV. 1–6)

In the first section we read that, under Moses, Sihon and Og were conquered and their land eventually given to Reuben, Gad and half the tribe of Manasseh. Keeping Sihon and Og in the record would remind the Israelites in years to come that part of the nation of Israel lived east of the Jordan. They could not cut them off, for they were part of God's people. We too may not cut off, despise or neglect those who differ from us. God has some very dear children but he has some very queer ones, too! If they are part of the body of Christ, however, they, together with us, are all one in Christ Jesus.

It would seem that these two and a half tribes east of Jordan soon lost their unique identity as Israelites. They seem to have been absorbed into the surrounding nations which they were supposed to overcome. Their buffer-zone location made them extremely vulnerable to both military attack and ungodly influence. Dangerous place, the borderlands. They are Satan's battleground and the scene of peril for those Christians who live in the borders of the world and threshold of the Kingdom. They can be enticed into forbidden alliances with a godless world.

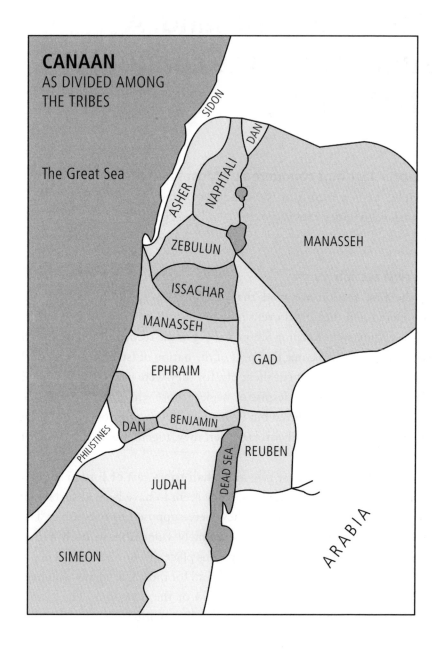

CANAAN
AS DIVIDED AMONG
THE TRIBES

The Great Sea

SIDON

DAN

ASHER

NAPHTALI

ZEBULUN

MANASSEH

ISSACHAR

MANASSEH

EPHRAIM

GAD

PHILISTINES

DAN

BENJAMIN

DEAD SEA

REUBEN

JUDAH

ARABIA

SIMEON

THE SECOND SECTION (VV. 7–24)

In the second section thirty-one kings are listed as having been conquered by Joshua in the land of Canaan. This proves that there had been a complete fulfilment of God's promise to Abram: 'To your descendants I will give this land' (Genesis 12:7). God was true to his word, and now we have the evidence listed before us! God is faithful. He gave them the land.

God will perform whatever he has promised! As we survey the years that have passed, we find that God has been so faithful! His eventual conquest is in sight! Soon we will be with that great throng praising the God who brought it all to pass, bringing us into the eternal land of rest with him—as he said he would!

Chapter 13: Geographical boundaries east of Jordan

Chapter 13 is the story of the division of the land east of Jordan and its distribution to the two and a half tribes mentioned above, but first it describes the unconquered parts of Canaan (vv. 1–7).

THE FIRST SECTION (VV. 1–7)

This first section tells us of the aging of Joshua, the assessment of Canaan, the divine promise of help and the assignment of work—God's command to Joshua to divide the land. Joshua was to superintend the allotting of the land to Israel. There were pockets of resistance which were to be dealt with by the individual tribes in their specific regions.

The chapter begins by recording that the Lord said to Joshua, 'You are old, advanced in years, and there remains very much land yet to be possessed' (v. 1). Joshua would have been at least as old as Caleb, who at this stage was eighty-five (14:10). He (Joshua) was one hundred and ten years old at the time of his death (24:29), so therefore would probably have been between ninety and one hundred years old at this stage—and God was still speaking to him!

Let not the old people think that they have no further contribution to make, for if they are in touch with God, their lives and words can be a tremendous blessing.

Here we see, firstly, that the statement in verse 1 ('You are old, advanced in years, and there remains very much land yet to be possessed') was not a rebuke but rather a tender acknowledgement that Joshua was but dust and that, although he had accomplished much, there was still much to be done. It was an *instructing* word. Secondly, this was a *humbling* word, for the enemy was still in possession of many parts of the country. Thirdly, it was an *exhorting* word; there was much more that needed to be done. He had to press on to further achievements. Fourthly, it was an *inspiring* word, for it was to remind him of his duty to divide the land so that the Israelites could root out its inhabitants.

The task of dividing the land was not nearly as rigorous as leading the armies into battle. When God's servants are enfeebled, he does not encourage them to be slack but assigns them lighter tasks. 'They shall still bear fruit in old age' (Psalm 92:14). The decay of nature is no reason why grace should languish.

God says, 'I will drive out [the residents of the land] from before the children of Israel' (v. 6). We are to be inspired to action by the promises of God. We are not to wait for God to do something for us when he expects us to be involved. We 'are workers together with him' (2 Corinthians 6:1).

The land was before them. It was not for them to stay forever in their comfort zones—Gilgal and later Shiloh (18:1). They had received an inheritance and it was now for them to possess their possessions. Their inheritance was the land; our inheritance is Christ. What the land was to them, Christ is to us. The possibilities of the life in Christ are endless. There is so much to possess. Paul says, '... that I may know him and the power of his resurrection, and the fellowship of his sufferings, being conformed to his death ... I press toward the goal for the prize of the upward call of God in Christ Jesus' (Philippians 3:10,14).

To know him we must find him in *his Word*. How few take time with the

Word of God! How many of its pages are unexplored territory, unclaimed possessions! Whole areas of the Word, which are there for us to discover and feed upon, are left unpossessed. We need to venture into areas which will yield sacred treasures as we begin to understand scriptural truths.

To know him is to *become Christ-like*, 'to be conformed to the image of his Son' (Romans 8:29). What characterized Jesus? We read that he 'did no sin'; 'in him is no sin'. He is the sinless Son of God. To be conformed to his image, therefore, we are to be 'holy and without blame before him in love' (Ephesians 1:4). Think of his holiness, think of his self-sacrifice and of his dedication to the will of God; think of his zeal, his love. Jesus my Lord! Wonderful Saviour!

To be like Jesus, To be like Jesus,
All I want is to be like him.

But to be like him we will have to be indwelt and possessed by him, so that his life may shine out of our lives. That means cleansing and transparency. It is only as we are totally yielded to him, cleansed by his precious blood, possessed, controlled and motivated by the Holy Spirit, that we are able to abide in his fullness, reach up in faith and claim the qualities of the One who has redeemed us. Oh, to know God, and to follow on to know him till he breaks through upon us and melts our hearts in his presence! What wonder there is in the revelation of his character, his loveliness! We bow before him in adoration and worship. How little do we possess of his beauty, his patience, his joy, his tenderness, his compassion, his holiness! But there where we meet him with broken hearts we are changed by his gracious power and love into the image of the One whom we adore! We begin to possess the land—our land, even Jesus.

If our hearts are not purged from selfish attitudes and interests, we will not be able to find the riches of our inheritance in him. Our peace will be broken by the raids of unremoved evil within us, which will swoop down from time to time and carry all before it. We will be distracted by that which we have allowed to live within us.

So many are saved and stuck! We are far from being conformed to his image. Let us ask our heavenly Joshua to settle us in the land, so that there may be no hill or dale that is not possessed. God help us to possess our possessions!

THE SECOND SECTION (VV. 8–33)

The second section describes the geographical boundaries of Reuben, Gad and half the tribe of Manasseh, all of whom settled east of Jordan. It spells out the recipe for disaster in verse 13: 'Nevertheless the children of Israel did not drive out the Geshurites or the Maachathites, but the Geshurites and the Maachathites dwell among the Israelites until this day.' 'They were unfaithful to the God of their fathers, and played the harlot after the gods of the peoples of the land, whom God had destroyed before them. So the God of Israel stirred up the spirit of ... Tiglath-Pileser king of Assyria. He carried the Reubenites, the Gadites, and the half-tribe of Manasseh into captivity' (1 Chronicles 5:25–26). The tragic end to their settlement was that they became like all the nations, worshipping the gods of the heathen. They who claimed their inheritance first were the first to lose it. Woe to those who dabble with the world and its deceitful friendship. How quickly they lose the cutting edge of their testimony and then drift far from God in bondage to the powers which the world exerts!

The Levites

Four times in these chapters we are reminded that the Levites were given no inheritance in the land (13:14,33; 14:3–4; 18:7). 'The sacrifices of the LORD God of Israel made by fire are their inheritance, as he said to them' (13:14). The priests and Levites received certain portions of the sacrifices as their due, as well as special tithes and offerings that the congregation were to bring. They were in the service of God, and the work of God was to carry them and provide for them. People would give and from those gifts the Levites would be supported and would live. This principle holds true while time lasts. 'Those who preach the gospel should live from the gospel' (1 Corinthians 9:14). 'The labourer is worthy of his wages' (Luke 10:7).

There were two reasons for this system being instituted. Firstly, God did not want the responsibilities and activities relating to tribal affairs to distract the Levites from their spiritual duties. They were to 'serve the Lord without distraction' (1 Corinthians 7:35).

Secondly, the Levites, while they had no geographical boundaries, would be living in the forty-eight cities with their lands allotted to them in different parts of the country (Numbers 35:1–8), and would be a decided influence for good wherever they were placed, for they would be accessible to the people.

We read that 'the LORD separated the tribe of Levi ... to stand before the LORD to minister to him and to bless in his name' (Deuteronomy 10:8). They were called to a life of worship ('to minister to him'), and to a life of service ('to bless in his name'). Their inheritance was not land but the Lord. They were held in high esteem and great honour. They would be able to teach the people the law of God, and their consecrated lives would spread spirituality throughout the land.

Is God separating you to his service? There is a precious, inward relationship with God which lies at the heart of all external work for him. For any work to be effective there must be a purity within, a brokenness of spirit, a fervent devotion, a vibrant prayer life. This precious communion is the heart of all ministry. Here my devotion will burn at white heat. My relationship with God is everything—everything! From this flows service for God. Commitment and love to God precede activity for God. Jesus said to Peter, 'Do you love me? ... Feed my sheep' (John 21:17). Active service came from devotion and love to the Lord Jesus. Oh, to fall in love with him! Then we would do his bidding with great joy, and our hearts would be captive to do his will whatever the cost and wherever he leads.

Balaam (13:22)

Since the tribe of Reuben had taken its territory from Moab, and since the story of Balaam was connected with the Moabites (Numbers 22–24), it is fitting that Balaam is mentioned here with the description of Reuben's territory. The Moabites were 'sick with dread because of the children of Israel' (Numbers 22:3), so Balak the king of Moab sent for Balaam to come and curse the invading Israelites, promising him great riches. With God on his lips and mammon in his heart, self-willed, he went. But instead of cursing the Israelites, he blessed them.

Seeing that he was failing in his prophecies, Balaam advised Balak to befriend the Israelites, to invite them to their feasts and to weaken them by compromise (Numbers 31:16). This resulted in some of the Jewish men taking Moabite women for themselves and violating the law of God. What Balaam failed to achieve by direct confrontation, he achieved by evil counsel, deceiving Israel into wicked compromises. We read of 'the counsel of Balaam' (Numbers 31:16)—his *counsel*; 'the way of Balaam' (2 Peter 2:15)—his *covetousness*; 'the error of Balaam' (Jude 11)—his *corruption*; 'the doctrine of Balaam' (Revelation 2:14)—his *compromise*.

The story of Balaam will ever be a warning against greed and compromise with the known will of God. This record in Joshua 13 tells us that 'the children of Israel ... killed with the sword Balaam the son of Beor, the soothsayer' (v. 22). He who attempted to destroy Israel was himself destroyed by Israel.

Chapters 15–19: The inheritances of the nine and a half tribes

Here is a summary of the inheritances of the tribes west of Jordan. The boundaries are given and many cities are named:

- Judah (15:1–63);
- Ephraim (16:4–10);
- Manasseh (17:1–13);
- Benjamin (18:11–28);

- Simeon (19:1–9);
- Zebulun (19:10–16);
- Issachar (19:17–23);
- Asher (19:24–31);
- Naphtali (19:32–39);
- Dan (19:40–48).

In many instances we read that they 'could not drive them out', for example in 15:63 and 17:12–13. This was a profound mistake on the part of Israel. They tolerated the Canaanites and lived beside them, allowing their corrupt influence to infiltrate the ranks of Israel. The Jebusites remained in Jerusalem until many years later, when David drove them out.

THE CASE OF ZELOPHEHAD'S DAUGHTERS (17:3–4)

Zelophehad had five daughters but no sons. That meant that there was no one to carry on his name through an inheritance in the land. They had gone to Moses and laid this problem before him. Moses had gone to God and he had given a ruling that the inheritance of the father should pass to the daughters (Numbers 27:1–8).

When Joshua began dividing the land, they reminded him of that which Moses had ruled. As in the case of Caleb, they based their request on the word of God. Joshua acted in accordance with this word and 'gave them an inheritance among their father's brothers'. This surely is a model as to how problems should be solved. Bring the matter to the spiritual leaders, who will lay the matter before God. Of course, we have here people who were not already biased towards a certain line of action, but were open to receive what God would give them and to implement it. May God give us such leaders!

THE COMPLAINT OF MANASSEH (17:7–18)

Half the tribe of Manasseh was settled to the east of Jordan, and now the other half, on the west of Jordan, complained, 'Why have you given us only one lot and one share to inherit, since we are a great people, inasmuch as the LORD has blessed us until now?' (v. 14). This was the only complaint about the allotments. The complaint was *unreasonable*. It was also *unjustifiable*, for the children of Joseph had been given three lots, one for Ephraim, one for half the tribe of Manasseh to the east of Jordan, and now this one west of Jordan. The complaint was also *proud*: 'We are a great people.' They wanted to be the dominant tribe. This type of person complains, spreading discontent, and damaging the cause of Christ.

Joshua's reply was incisive and scathing. He argued with intense sarcasm, 'If you are a great people, then go up to the forest country and clear a place for yourself there' (v. 15). He focused on the responsibility of greatness, not on its privilege. It was a cutting rebuke.

They replied that, even should they do that, the land would still not be enough for them. Joshua himself was of the tribe of Ephraim (Numbers 13:8), but he was not swayed by selfish interests. They probably hoped that he would promote his own tribe, but he declined to show favouritism. He replied that they should cut down the wooded area for more land, and that they should 'drive out the Canaanites' (v. 18); but they 'did not utterly drive them out' (v. 13).

If we are lazy and self-indulgent we cannot hope to be enriched by that which is freely offered to us in the gospel. May God help us to do with our might that which he has bid us do! Joshua comes out of this episode with flying colours. Again he is seen to be a man of great integrity and fairness—a worthy leader.

SHILOH (18:1)

Joshua set up the tabernacle of meeting at Shiloh, which means 'peace' or 'rest', 'And the land was subdued before them' (18:1). The tabernacle was pitched as nearly as possible in the centre of the country. This remained the centre of Israelite worship until the days of Eli. Jesus is the centre of worship for his people. Around him we gather. He is the heart of all true worship.

It is probable that, because Shiloh was central, the tabernacle was placed there to make it more convenient for the men to go there during the annual festivals, for Gilgal was at the extremity of the land. They 'assembled together at Shiloh, and set up the tabernacle of meeting there' (18:1).

JOSHUA'S INHERITANCE (19:49–51)

Notice the *timing* of the gift. It surely is the mark of a great and humble leader to wait for all the others to receive their inheritances first before being given his. Selfless Joshua waited for all the others to receive theirs first.

Notice also the *transparency* of the gift: 'The children of Israel gave an inheritance among them to Joshua' (v. 49). He received it in an official way. It was approved by the public. There was nothing underhand. No one could say that he used his position to manipulate his allocation.

The *touchstone* and basis of the gift was the word of God: 'According to the word of the LORD they gave him the city which he asked for' (v. 50). We have no record of the giving of this word by God, but this gift must have been based upon the promise of the Lord. The people were glad for him to have it.

Notice the *testimony* of the man. Joshua 'built the city and dwelt in it' (v. 50). Unlike those of the tribe of Manasseh, Joshua laboured, despite the fact that he was an old man, and he established his inheritance. He was responsible and faithful to the last.

Notice finally the *typology* of the inheritance. He asked for the city, built it and lived in it, just as our heavenly Joshua receives 'his inheritance in the saints' (Ephesians 1:18), builds his church and dwells therein.

Chapter 21: The inheritance of the Levites

Chapter 21 deals with the cities assigned to the Levites: the Kohathites, the Gershonites and the Merarites. There were forty-eight cities, six of which were cities of refuge. We know that there were 23,000 Levites before Israel entered the land (Numbers 26:62), so it was a great number to place among forty-eight cities. The Levite cities were so placed that no one was too far away to be able to receive help from the Levites. 'So the LORD gave to Israel all the land of which he had sworn to give to their fathers … Not a word failed of any good thing which the LORD had spoken to the house of Israel. All came to pass' (21:43,45).

Caleb (14:6–15; 15:13–19)

aleb is one of the great characters in the Bible: a man of vibrant
faith and daring courage. He has been worthily described as Mr
Greatheart of the Old Testament.

We find the account of Caleb in two parts. The first part appears in 14:6–
15, and the second part in 15:13–19. His words and deeds are recorded only
here and in Numbers 13–14, where he was described as a representative of
the tribe of Judah sent to spy out the land. He and Joshua were the only two
who returned to Kadesh Barnea with a favourable report. Of Caleb God
said, 'My servant Caleb, because he has a different spirit in him and has
followed me fully, I will bring into the land where he went, and his
descendants shall inherit it' (Numbers 14:24).

With the exception of Joshua, Caleb was the oldest man in all Israel, for
all who were above twenty years of age when he was forty died in the
wilderness. He and Joshua were the sole survivors of their generation,
which had left Egypt. He was therefore at least twenty years older than any
of the others.

He is here called 'the Kenizzite'. Keil and Delitzsch say, 'We are not to
understand that Caleb or his father Jephunneh is described as a descendant
of the Canaanitish tribe of the Kenezzites (Genesis 15:19), but Kenaz was a
descendant of Hezron, the son of Perez and grandson of Judah.'[1] Given
that he was a 'leader' of the tribe of Judah (Numbers 13:2) just after they
had left Egypt, it seems improbable that he could have been a foreigner, as
some claim, for the qualities and positions of leadership would have
evolved among the children of Israel while they were still in Egypt and at
Sinai. It would seem, therefore, that Caleb was an Israelite and a leader of
the tribe of Judah.

Joshua's great leadership qualities and his deeds are well documented, but we hear nothing of Caleb, who simply took his place once more in the tribe of Judah. Now, as an old man of eighty-five, he comes before his leader and former spy partner, Joshua, and reminds him of what Moses had said to him when he sent them both out to investigate the land: 'The land where your foot has trodden shall be your inheritance' (Joshua 14:9). The grand old man was claiming an inheritance. This hill country was occupied by the mighty Anakim, before whom the ten spies had seen themselves as grasshoppers. He asked Joshua for mountains to climb and giants to conquer! Mr Greatheart cries out, 'Give me this mountain!' What a word of faith and inspiration!

He brought 'the children of Judah' (14:6), that is the heads of his tribe, with him to testify their consent to his claim. God chose him from Judah to divide the land (Numbers 34:18–19) so, lest he should seem to be improving his lot for personal advantage as a commissioner, he brings them with him to give their approval.

Caleb was a man of vibrant faith

'Without faith it is impossible to please [God]' (Hebrews 11:6). Caleb had a robust and unwavering faith that was all the more remarkable because it was surrounded by the gigantic waves of unbelief arising from the opposition of those who chose to believe the pessimistic reports of the ten spies.

HE BELIEVED IN GOD'S PURPOSES

'He brought us out from there, that he might bring us in, to give us the land of which he swore to our fathers' (Deuteronomy 6:23). That was the object of their leaving Egypt—to enter into their rightful inheritance promised to Abraham and given to them by God. Caleb knew that Joseph had said on his deathbed, 'God will surely visit you, and bring you out of this land to the land of which he swore to Abraham, to Isaac, and to Jacob.' Joseph had then charged the people: 'You shall carry up my bones from here' (Genesis

50:24–25). The bones of Joseph were an inspiration to faith and an indication of God's purposes for the nation.

He had been brought out of Egypt by God's power. There was purpose in God's miraculous care and provision in the wilderness. God did not guide them by the cloud and fiery pillar in order to leave them at the mercy of this howling wilderness or of the giants occupying the land. God was saying to them, 'Go up and possess the land.' This miracle-working God intended to give them the land, and they were to obey him and take it. It all made sense to Caleb.

HE TRUSTED IN GOD'S PROMISES

His was a faith founded upon the word of God. He remembered the time and place of God's speaking to him. Several times in his request to Joshua, Caleb mentions God's word: 'the word which the LORD said to Moses the man of God' (14:6); 'as he said' (v. 10a); 'ever since the LORD spoke this word to Moses' (v. 10b); 'which the LORD spoke in that day' (v. 12a); 'as the LORD said' (v. 12b). Five times Caleb hammers this point home. He bases his request on the word which the Lord had spoken to Moses, and this request is for nothing other than that which God promised him. He simply believed God. For Caleb, God was able to give glorious victory against overwhelming odds! 'Now therefore,' he said, 'give me this mountain of which the LORD spoke in that day' (v. 12). He claimed the promise. It was an unwavering faith in the face of massive opposition in the land. 'Give me this mountain'—a striking and grand watchword for us all!

The ten measured their own strength against that of the giants, and the two, Joshua and Caleb, measured the giants against God. The ten gazed at the giants; the two gazed at God. The ten had great giants and a small God; the two had a great God and small giants. God was far greater than these giant people in their strong fortified cities. Caleb remembered gratefully what God had done when 'Israel wandered in the wilderness' (v. 10). He said, 'He will bring us into this land and give it to us ... Only do not rebel against the LORD, nor fear the people of the land, for they are our bread; their protection has departed from them, and the LORD is with us. Do not fear them' (Numbers 14:8–9). As one commentator put it, 'they are our bread' means 'the bigger the giant, the bigger the loaf'. We will consume them!

This magnificent blending of faith and courage failed to elicit any response among the people. Sadly, Caleb was being introduced to the isolation of faith. He and Joshua stood alone and pleaded with the rebellious multitudes, who 'said to stone them with stones' (Numbers 14:10). It was a great national mutiny. God banished them to the wilderness, and all those who were twenty years or above when they left Egypt died in the wilderness. The spies had spent forty days in the land, and unbelieving Israel's sentence was forty years in the wilderness: a year for a day (Numbers 14:29,33–34).

HE RELIED ON GOD'S PRESENCE

'The LORD is with us!' he cried (Numbers 14:9). Full of expectancy he said to Joshua, 'It may be that the LORD will be with me, and I shall be able to drive them out as the LORD said' (Joshua 14:12). 'As the LORD said' shows that his trust was in the Lord and that this was a word of confidence. Because of *Yahweh*'s promise, such as that in Exodus 23:29–31, Caleb suspects that *Yahweh* will drive out the enemy before him. He is expectant, not doubtful; confident, not cocky; for God is with him.

How precious is the presence of God! How humbling, how encouraging, how inspiring! As we wait in his presence, far from the madding crowd's ignoble strife, his radiant beauty meets our sight and Jesus fills the horizon. We are encompassed in his tender embrace as he touches our deepest heart-strings. We bow and weep and repeat his wonderful Name as our hearts are melted before him. He ravishes our soul; he fills the horizon; he is the altogether Lovely One. There is nothing like the presence of God. With God's presence we can go through fire and water. God said to Moses, 'My

Presence will go with you, and I will give you rest.' Then Moses replied, 'If your Presence does not go with us, do not bring us up from here' (Exodus 33:14–15). In his presence the fire burns fiercely in our hearts and our commitment is total. Complete abandonment to him and his will is so easy when we find the wonder of the Lord in the precious trysting-place.

HE WAS CONFIDENT OF GOD'S POWER

Caleb had witnessed God in action. He had seen so much of the power of God. He had gazed upon the river of Egypt which turned to blood, he had heard the wailing of the Egyptians when they realized that their firstborn were dead. Ah, yes, he knew that God was alive and was the all-powerful One. He had walked together with all the others across the dry seabed. He had seen Pharaoh and his hordes drown in the waters as they pursued Israel. He had eaten the manna in the camp of Israel. He had seen enemy forces, like those of Amalek, defeated. He knew that if God was with him he would be victorious. If God be for us, who can be against us?

How little we know of the power of God in our lives and in our meetings! We see so little of the melting presence of God, so little of brokenness. How we need God to reveal his power and his presence, which will most certainly transform our lives and enable us to go forth and conquer! 'The people who know their God shall be strong, and carry out great exploits' (Dan. 11:32).

Caleb was a man with a consistent life

A number of qualities marked his character:

PHYSICAL STRENGTH

He said, 'The LORD has kept me alive' (Joshua 14:10). That was no ordinary statement. He had watched a whole generation die in the wilderness. In fact, he and Joshua were the only ones to have survived. He probably had had many scrapes with death in the battles for the land.

Through it all, 'the LORD has kept me alive'. That speaks of agility, strength, watchfulness and alertness. He was no slouch. He was awake, able, active and available.

He said, 'I am as strong this day as on the day that Moses sent me; just as my strength was then, so now is my strength for war' (14:11). He said these things as if anticipating objections to his propositions because of his age. It is surely a wonderful testimony to God's keeping power and sustaining grace. The old man, who should have been putting on his slippers, ties on his mountain boots and prepares for an all-out war. He is up for the most difficult of tasks. His trust is in God, who would give him the victory. What a spirit! What spiritual initiative and drive!

DAUNTLESS COURAGE

This courage was both moral and physical. Morally, he had stood almost alone against the swiftly-flowing tide of popular opinion. Standing alone is one of the most searching tests, particularly for young people. It takes courage to stand alone.

Physically, he had held firmly to his convictions even when the despairing, menacing crowd cried out to stone him to death. He had advised a dangerous line of action, that of attacking the Canaanites, and when he later claimed his inheritance he claimed the very mountainous area that was infested with hordes of fierce Anakim in their fortified cities. It would seem that this was the place from which the spies had concluded that the conquest of the land was impossible, for Hebron seemed altogether invincible. This was the very place that Caleb claimed. It took courage, but this rose from his unshakeable trust in his great God.

SELFLESSNESS

Caleb had lived quietly, seeking no particular honour for himself. His choice of Hebron was not only courageous but also unselfish. Would it not have been easier for Caleb to ask for some well-conquered and productive fertile valley, where he could spend the rest of his days in peaceful enjoyment? But no! Selflessly, courageously and believingly he offers to drive out the Anakim from their fortified cities and preserve the area for himself and for the nation.

When Joshua was promoted as leader, Caleb accepted the choice and was happy to follow his new leader. He was not even made second-in-command. We read of no attitude of jealousy or chafing under the guidance and command of Joshua. He selflessly accepted his lot and willingly served in his appointed place.

STEADFASTNESS

Caleb had been so convinced that God was with them at Kadesh Barnea, but how did he fare in the long, tedious years of wilderness wandering? The testings of the long haul take their toll. Unconsciously, deterioration sets in, and the one who was so bright in youth often fails in middle life. Don't lose heart and lose the vision in midlife!

For forty years he was with the complaining, unbelieving and dying multitude wandering aimlessly in the desert. This is where his trust in God had brought him! Yet he did not become resentful, but maintained his spiritual integrity. He survived the long test without losing stature. He was in the commonplace, the humdrum, for so long, but his commitment remained as fresh as ever and his devotion just as vital.

WHOLEHEARTED DEVOTION

The secret of Caleb's life is found in the phrase which is repeated five times in these chapters: 'He wholly followed the LORD' (Joshua 14:8–9,14; Numbers 14:24; 32:12; Deuteronomy 1:36). Caleb himself states, 'I wholly followed the LORD' (Joshua 14:8). This is an honest declaration of an undeflected purpose. Moses said to him, 'You have wholly followed the LORD my God' (Joshua 14:9). And God testified, 'Caleb ... has followed me fully' (Numbers 14:24).

Here is a man of unbending integrity, who followed the Lord through thick and thin. When his life was in danger from the stones of his disgruntled brethren, he stood firm; when he walked the weary paths in the wilderness, all because the nation had rejected what he knew to be true, he stood firm; when the army invaded Canaan, he gave himself to the battles; when the biggest challenge of all faced him, that of conquering the mighty mountainous region of Hebron, he was there to meet the challenge. He followed God wholeheartedly and with complete abandon. He entertained no divided loyalties. He was committed to God's person, whom he would serve, and to his will, which he would do.

Caleb was a man with a wide inheritance

Not only did Caleb claim and possess his inheritance of the hill country centred in Hebron, but God blessed him in so many other ways as well.

HE HAD A LONG LIFE

When God told Joshua that he was old, Caleb was still full of the vigour of youth. God had strengthened him to fulfil his purposes so that at the last he could drive the giants from the land.

HE HAD CONTINUED STRENGTH AND OPPORTUNITY FOR SERVICE

The best reward for service is further service. He was in superb condition physically and would not only conquer the Anakim but would also be involved in the organization of the new settlement in Hebron. His service continued. It is often the case that the greatest of all of life's achievements take place in old age. It's not too late to reach out for God's best! Caleb trusted in what God had said to him. He increased in stature until the end. The best was always yet to be!

HE CLAIMED HIS POSSESSION

Arba was the greatest man among the Anakim (Joshua 14:15), and he gave his name to the city (Hebron), which was formerly called Kirjath Arba. His son Anak had three sons, Sheshai, Ahiman and Talmai, and Caleb drove out these men from Hebron (15:13–14). Caleb conquered! Hebron was fruitful, for rich produce came in from the nearby fertile areas.

HE HAD REST

'Then the land had rest from war' (14:15). The name 'Hebron' conveys the meaning of friendship, love and communion. At last Caleb could share in the rest together with the whole land. It had been a long battle, but at last there was rest.

HIS FAITH AND SPIRIT WERE INFECTIOUS

Kirjath Sepher lay just south of Hebron—later to be called Debir. Caleb threw out the challenge, 'He who attacks Kirjath Sepher and takes it, to him I will give Achsah my daughter as wife' (15:16). Othniel rose in his strength, took the city and claimed his bride. She had dry land, so she took the initiative and asked her father, '"Give me also springs of water." So he gave her the upper springs and the lower springs' (15:19). The land could now be irrigated and would be useful and productive. Caleb's spirit spilled over into his children, and they too were able to reach out to claim their inheritance in the fruitful area around Hebron. He made sure that his daughter had a worthy husband. Othniel later became the judge of Israel (Judges 3:10).

Note

1 **C. F. Keil and F. Delitzsch,** *Commentary on the Old Testament*, Vol. 2 (Grand Rapids: Eerdmans, 1978), p. 148.

Cities of refuge (20:1–9)

J oshua now appointed six cities of refuge. They were all Levitical cities; in other words, the provision of mercy had something to do with God! There were three on the west of Jordan and three on the east. On the west there were Kedesh to the north, Shechem in the centre of the land, and Hebron in the south. On the east there were Golan in the north, Ramoth in Gilead in the centre, and Bezer in the south.

If a person was judged to have committed a premeditated murder, capital punishment would ensue; but if he killed someone by accident, then he would have the privilege of seeking protection in a city of refuge. Anyone who killed a person unintentionally could flee to the gate of the nearest city of refuge and the avenger of blood, the relative of the dead person assigned to exact punishment, could not harm him. He would be assessed, and if he were not guilty of murder, would be given asylum in the city. The cities of refuge were within reach of all the children of Israel as well as of 'the stranger who dwelt among them' (v. 9). No harm would come to the manslayer if he stayed in the city until the death of the high priest, after which he could return to his own community as a free man.

This is rich in typical teaching, for we see ourselves to be among those who are condemned for the sins which we have committed. Should death, the avenger of blood, find us outside the City of Refuge, eternal destruction will result. Awakened to our need, we flee to the place of mercy. We have no means by which we can save ourselves and we are in fearful danger of judgement. We are being pursued by the wrath of a righteous God. We flee to our City of Refuge, even Jesus. Fleeing for refuge implies fleeing from sin; seeing it and repenting of it.

This emphasizes the responsibility of the sinner, for, while a provision has been made for sinners to escape the wrath of the avenger of blood, they

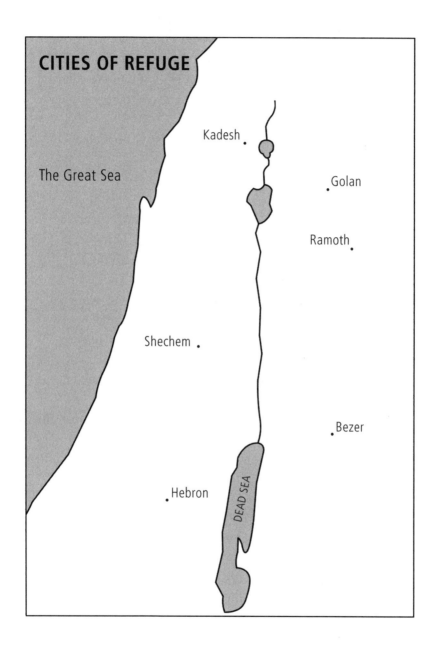

must avail themselves of it. It would be wrong for them to say, 'I suppose that I am ordained to perish. I am elected to die.' They are to flee to the place of mercy which God has provided for them. If you are outside of God's gracious provision for you in Christ, then I implore you to flee to him for mercy. If you do not, the judgement will overtake you and you will perish. Flee from the impending judgement!

Elijah said, 'How long will you falter between two opinions? If the LORD is God, follow him' (1 Kings 18:21). The people then had to choose, and follow that choice with actions. Joshua said, 'Choose for yourselves this day whom you will serve' (Joshua 24:15). That was something they had to do. Jesus said, 'Come to me' (Matthew 11:28). He will save us, but he can do nothing for us until we come. We have to come! The woman with the flow of blood had to press through the crowd to touch the hem of Jesus' garment. Had she but wished for her healing it would not have happened (Matthew 9:21–22). Jesus said to the man with the withered hand, '"Stretch out your hand." And he stretched it out, and his hand was restored as whole as the other' (Mark 3:5). As he stretched out his hand, the healing took place. There is divine sovereignty, but there is also human responsibility. God extends mercy, but we are to come and receive that mercy.

Two passages in the New Testament evidently refer to the cities of refuge: '… found in him, not having my own righteousness' (Philippians 3:9); and '… we might have strong consolation, who have fled for refuge to lay hold of the hope set before us' (Hebrews 6:18).

The cities of refuge are a type of Christ as he is offered to sinners in the gospel.

They were *appointed by God himself*. God appointed Christ to be the Saviour of sinners.

The cities were appointed to *provide shelter from the avenger*. No one can defy divine justice. 'Today, if you will hear his voice, do not harden your hearts' (Hebrews 3:15).

The cities were *easily seen*, being built on hills or mountains. This made them more readily accessible. 'Him God has exalted to his right hand to be Prince and Saviour, to give repentance to Israel and forgiveness of sins' (Acts 5:31).

The road to the city was *plainly marked*. 'You shall prepare roads … that any manslayer may flee there' (Deuteronomy 19:3). Roads to the cities were clearly signposted. The gospel must be faithfully declared, that all may know the way.

There was *ease of access*. When someone had need of one, it was near at hand. A city of refuge could be reached within a day's journey from anywhere in the land. 'The LORD is near to those who have a broken heart, and saves such as have a contrite spirit' (Psalm 34:18).

The city of refuge provided protection from the avenger of blood *only for the manslayer*. The deliberate murderer was excluded. There is no salvation in Christ for those deliberately continuing in sin. Those who reject the offer of God's mercy exclude themselves from his salvation. In Christ the penitent sinner is safe from the fury of a raging devil, from the pain of a guilty conscience, and from the wrath of a holy God.

The one who took refuge in the city of mercy *had to remain there*. If he left the protection of the city, the avenger of blood had the right to find him and kill him (Numbers 35:26–27). Having come to Christ, we are to abide in him.

The cities were *available to Gentiles as well as to Jews*. Christ's salvation is universal. 'There is no distinction between Jew and Greek' (Romans 10:12).

It was the *death of the high priest* which secured a full and final deliverance. In the death of our High Priest, Jesus Christ, our salvation is accomplished. We are safe in the city and saved by his death.

The names of the cities *speak of salvation*. Kedesh means 'holy'; Christ is made to the believer sanctification and righteousness (1 Corinthians 1:30). Shechem means 'shoulder', the place of strength and safety; in Christ the believer finds security. Hebron means 'fellowship', and through Christ we are brought into fellowship with him. Bezer means 'a fortified place', and God is our refuge and fortress (Psalm 91:2). Ramoth means 'height' or 'exaltation', and in Christ we are made to sit in heavenly places (Ephesians 2:6). Golan means 'exultation' or 'joy', and we 'rejoice in God through our Lord Jesus Christ' (Romans 5:11).

What a powerful relevance these cities of refuge have for us today!

A dangerous misunderstanding (22:1–34)

In the last three chapters of the book Joshua has three counselling sessions. The first is with the soldiers of the two and a half tribes (22:1–9); the second (ch. 23) and third (ch. 24) are with Israel in the land. In chapter 22 Joshua speaks to the soldiers of the tribes who had settled in Transjordan and who had been away from their wives and families for seven years. They had completed their obligation to help with the conquest of the land. There were some 40,000 of them (4:12–13). Joshua now gathers them together to give them words of commendation and advice before they set off for their homes.

Having received Joshua's blessing they journeyed eastwards, and when they came to the Jordan they built an altar to commemorate their oneness with the nine and a half tribes west of the Jordan, so that future generations would not regard them as being separate from Israel.

The building of the altar was reported to the tribes in Canaan, who became so indignant that they were ready to go to war immediately with the tribes east of the Jordan for what they perceived to be treachery in forsaking the Lord. A delegation was sent to them and accusations were made. They gave adequate and acceptable explanations, which brought peace and averted a violent civil war.

First we see the counselling session with the two and a half tribes at Shiloh.

The commendation and admonition (vv. 1–9)
JOSHUA COMMENDED THEIR PERFORMANCE (VV. 1–3)
It was a tribute of high praise, and coming from their general, it would have been most heartening for the tribes to know that they had been

appreciated. They had performed their duties excellently. They had kept their promise to Moses. For seven years they had put the interests of the nation before their own comforts. Joshua recognized that they were men of their word and had kept 'all' that Moses had commanded them. Oh, for such integrity today!

Not only had they kept their promise to Moses, but they had also obeyed Joshua, who said that they had 'obeyed my voice in all that I commanded you' (v. 2). When Joshua had taken over the leadership he did not take for granted that they would carry out their obligations to Moses, so he had reminded the soldiers of those obligations (1:12–15). Their response had been immediate and wholehearted: 'All that you command us we will do, and wherever you send us we will go' (1:16). They did not simply follow personalities. Leaders may change, but it is the cause of Christ to which we are committed.

They were also faithful to their brethren. 'You have not left your brethren these many days, up to this day' (v. 3). They had endured the difficulties and dangers together with the others. They had stayed the course. How different to the Ephraimites we read of in the Psalms, who 'turned back in the day of battle' (Psalm 78:9–10).

Finally, they obeyed God. 'You … have kept … the commandment of the LORD your God' (v. 3).

What a great group of men these were! They were faithful, loyal, consecrated, submissive, obedient men of integrity and worth. Surely these qualities were derived from their relationship to the Lord, whose charge they kept. May we too merit such commendation at the end of the day.

JOSHUA DISCHARGED THEM FROM SERVICE (V. 4)

They had been on military duty in Canaan for seven years and now they were released from active duty. 'Return and go to your tents and to the land of your possession.' What relief and exhilaration this must have brought them! They could go home—to their wives and children!

There would probably not have been any great need for them after the battle at Hazor, but they had stayed. They had waited for their leader to take the initiative and demobilize them. Our appreciation of their obedience must soar, and also that of the personal qualities of Joshua, at whose word they remained.

JOSHUA COUNSELLED THEM TO LIVE RIGHTEOUSLY (VV. 5–6)

'Take careful heed to do the commandment and the law which Moses the servant of the LORD commanded you, to love the LORD your God, to walk in all his ways, to keep his commandments, to hold fast to him, and to serve him with all your heart and with all your soul' (v. 5).

This passage is a quotation from the book of Deuteronomy (6:5; 10:12; 11:13,22; 30:6,16,20). They were to 'hold fast to [God]', or 'cling to him'. Now that they would be far away from anyone checking on their behaviour, they were to be even more dedicated. They were to live under scriptural authority, live righteously and serve God wholeheartedly. The remarks are crowded together in order to impress their meaning on all of their hearts more deeply.

JOSHUA REWARDS THEM FOR THEIR SERVICE (VV. 7–8)

'Joshua blessed them.' What a way to end their period of service! They had his full approval and deep appreciation. Joshua then said, 'Return with much riches to your tents, with very much livestock, with silver, with gold, with bronze, with iron, and with very much clothing.' They were well-rewarded, and not only by the words from Joshua's mouth, for the blessing extended to practical things as well and they went home richly laden with great herds and much spoil. But Joshua was wise and fair to the last. He also said, 'Divide the spoil of your enemies with your brethren', that is, with their brethren who had stayed behind to guard the families and the belongings. Moses had established this principle long ago (Numbers 31:26–27). Each man would have his just portion. Joshua's character shines brightly every time we encounter him.

The construction of the altar (vv. 10–12)

On their way home, 'when they came to the region of the Jordan ... [they] built an altar there by the Jordan'. They feared lest in time to come the nine and a half tribes would say that they had no part in Israel, so they decided to build an altar of witness to assert their oneness with the rest of Israel. It was not an altar upon which they would offer any sacrifices, but one that would stand as a witness to their unity with the tribes west of Jordan. But it was a huge mistake. They had received no instructions from God to build.

It was well intended, but misunderstood. How often are the motives of the heart misread over perfectly innocent incidents! When they crossed the Jordan they had built a memorial altar on the banks of the river to commemorate the crossing, so it was perfectly natural to build another to commemorate their return. They built it, and were suddenly thrown into the teeth of a looming civil war.

God had instructed the nation that they were not to offer sacrifices on any altar but that which he had ordained at the tabernacle of meeting (Leviticus 17:8–9). This was no light matter. The construction of this unauthorized altar seemed to mean apostasy. The news spread quickly and alarm spread throughout the land. The Israelites gathered at Shiloh ready to go to war against their brethren. They had fought alongside these 40,000 men who had just left them and who had been so warmly commended by Joshua. They were their friends, their mates! But now they were prepared to fight against them! This is nothing but utter dedication to God. They would let nothing defile his honour! What they perceived as rebellion against God had to be dealt with quickly and severely.

The delegation (vv. 13–14)

The thorough investigation of the situation is admirable. Phinehas the son of Eleazar the priest was despatched with ten representative rulers to the eastern tribes, to discover the truth. The choice of Phinehas was a wise one. When Israel went a-whoring after the women of Moab at Peor, Phinehas had killed a man and a woman, thus stopping the plague which God sent (Numbers 25). His zeal for God was highly respected. If he were to judge the two and a half tribes to be blameless, it would be acceptable to the other tribes because of his reputation.

The investigation (vv. 15–20)

The tribes did not simply rush into war, but their representatives were carefully to examine the reason for this seemingly abominable act. They were to come to a righteous decision. Their questioning and exhortations continued at some length (vv. 15–20). In fact, they made them an offer to cross over the river and settle among the other tribes if necessary for the nation to be saved. This would, of course, create an enormous upheaval in the land which had already been divided and allocated to the various tribes. They would have to give up their lands and properties, but they would rather pay any price than see their brothers fall away from God. This shows a beautiful spirit of kindness, compassion, flexibility and maturity. Love, costly love, is that which wins people back to God.

The explanation (vv. 21–29)

The men of the departing tribes responded immediately and presented their case with simplicity, sincerity and clarity. They agreed with the charges and with the judgement: 'If it is in rebellion ... do not save us this day' (v. 22). But they denied that it was rebellion. They called upon God as their witness that they had not built the altar for burnt offerings or for sacrifices, but rather for future generations, as a witness to the fact that they were part of Israel. It was built not to be a functional altar but a memorial one. It was not an altar of division but of union.

The reconciliation (vv. 30–31)

The explanations given by the east of Jordan tribes were acceptable and pleasing to Phinehas and his delegation. 'This day we perceive that the

Lord is among us, because you have not committed this treachery against the Lord,' said Phinehas. It was a great relief. Armed conflict had been avoided! The bonds of brotherhood had been restored. They parted as brothers and friends.

The celebration (vv. 32–33)

Phinehas and the other leaders returned and brought back the news. 'So the thing pleased the children of Israel, and the children of Israel blessed God; they spoke no more of going against them in battle.' Open confrontation had been averted, and praise ascended to God.

The conclusion (v. 34)

The two and a half tribes called the altar *ed*, which means 'witness': 'For it is a witness between us that the Lord is God.' They were affirming their faith. How long they retained their faith we do not know, but we do know that they were carried away in bondage by the Assyrians some time later (1 Chronicles 5:25–26); a sad end to those who had pledged such allegiance.

Joshua's first farewell address (23:1–16)

oshua was old. At the end of the conquest he was about ninety years of age. At the time of his death he was one hundred and ten years old (24:29), so the 'long time after the LORD had given rest' (between chapters 22 and 23) would have been about twenty years. He now wanted to give a final charge to those who were to follow him.

The last words of a person's life take on special significance. They are not just casual remarks. Joshua, with a deep concern for the people, called the leaders of the nation together, either at Shiloh, the seat of the nation's government at that time (19:51), or at his own home in Ephraim. It was surely a memorable gathering for them, for his speech was full of gratitude towards God and full of warnings, counsel and admonitions to the leaders of the people.

His grateful acknowledgement (vv. 3–4,9,14)

Joshua begins by *giving praise to God*: 'You have seen all that the LORD your God has done.' He exalts God, and reminds them twice in verse 3 that he is 'the LORD *your* God'. In fact, in this chapter he is called 'the LORD your God' twelve times. Their wonderful God has given them the land as he said he would. Joshua reminds them that it is 'he who has fought for you'. He gave them victory after victory. God be praised and exalted!

GOD PUNISHED THE NATIONS

The cup of the nations' iniquity was full and God used Israel to exterminate the evil that was prevalent in the land. 'The LORD has driven out from before you great and strong nations' (v. 9).

GOD GAVE THEM A POSSESSION

Joshua says, 'I have divided to you by lot these nations that remain' (v. 4). They had an inheritance! Israel must now remember the source of her inheritance and that memory would serve to keep them from apostasy. God had given them the land.

GOD KEPT HIS PROMISES

'Not one thing has failed of all the good things which the LORD your God spoke concerning you. All have come to pass for you; not one word of them has failed' (v. 14). What a wonderful testimony to God's goodness and faithfulness! God be praised!

His glad anticipation (vv. 5, 10)

Joshua is also grateful for what God is doing now and what he will do for the nation in the future.

God's *promise* is ever there! 'And the LORD your God will expel them from before you ... So you shall possess their land, as the LORD your God promised you' (v. 5). In this verse he speaks twice of 'the LORD *your* God'. Joshua is impressing upon them the personal nature of this relationship. God in *person* is with them. Their God will continue to keep his promises and continue to fight for them. They can go forward in glad anticipation of victory in the companionship and inspiration of their God.

Joshua also speaks of God's *power*: 'One man of you shall chase a thousand' (v. 10). They will conquer and put their enemies to flight. This is a people blessed by God.

His great appeal (vv. 6–8, 11–13)

Joshua was desperately concerned that Israel did not slide into apostasy. He counselled them earnestly and warned them faithfully.

OBEDIENCE

His first announcement is very similar to that which he received at the beginning of his leadership in Joshua 1:6–8. Here he repeats the sentiments which have been his guiding light: 'Be very courageous to keep and to do all that is written in the Book of the Law of Moses' (v. 6). The word has led him through the battles and the conquests. He is passing on the torch. Be obedient to the word of God at all times! Take courage! Stand firm! They were to 'keep and ... do *all* that is written'. Half-hearted, partial or incomplete obedience is just not acceptable. Obedience must be complete and wholehearted.

SEPARATION

Joshua fears that Israel will merge with the heathen nations and fall into gross apostasy. He says that they must not *mingle* with the nations: '... and lest you go among these nations, these who remain among you' (v. 7). If they socialize together, it will result in a falling away from the living God. 'Have no fellowship with the unfruitful works of darkness' (Ephesians 5:11). Our strength lies not in mixing with the world but in separating from it. True, we must have friends and contacts who are not Christians, but to dabble in the world's godless affairs will damage our spiritual lives. Sadly, today there is an unholy mixed multitude which weakens the witness of the church.

Neither must they *worship* the gods of the nations: 'You shall not serve them nor bow down to them' (v. 7). He covers all aspects of involvement with the heathen religions. They were not to worship nor give place to that which could encourage such worship ('make mention of the name of their gods'), nor swear by them, thus giving them status and authority.

They must also not *marry* the heathen people: 'If indeed you ... make marriages with them ... know for certain that the LORD your God will no longer drive out these nations from before you' (vv. 12–13). Joshua echoed the words of Moses: 'Nor shall you make marriages with them'

(Deuteronomy 7:3). Spiritual compatibility is the primary qualification for marriage.

LOYALTY

'But you shall hold fast to the LORD your God' (v. 8). Here is a picture of steadfastness and loyalty. We have the picture of something firmly attached or glued to an object. This is how we should cleave or hold fast to the Lord.

LOVE

'Therefore take careful heed to yourselves, that you love the LORD your God' (v. 11). Again Joshua echoes Moses: 'You shall love the LORD your God with all your heart, with all your soul, and with all your strength' (Deuteronomy 6:5). When we have seen what Jesus did for us, his love conquers us and springs up within us. How can we be drawn away from our wonderful Saviour? Take heed—love the Lord your God! Love will hold you close to him—far more wonderful than anything that the world can offer!

His grave admonition (vv. 12–13,15–16)

If they go back and mingle with the heathen, 'know for certain that the LORD your God will no longer drive out these nations from before you. But they shall be snares and traps to you, and scourges on your sides and thorns in your eyes, until you perish' (v. 13). Know for certain! This judgement will most assuredly come! God will no longer be with them. There is a threat of *divine withdrawal* and a certainty of judgement if they turn away from God and embrace the doctrines and practices of the heathen. If they turn away from God, they will perish!

If God will no longer be with us, because we have turned to the world instead of towards him, we will lose our spirituality and will eventually disappear from the company of the people of God. Know for certain that this will happen.

If God is not fighting for them, the *menace of the heathen nations* will grow and they will be a scourge to them until they 'perish from this good land which the LORD your God has given you' (v. 13). You will learn to live as the heathen live until you are destroyed as a nation, for the principles of holiness received from God will have been swept away by the incoming flood of heathen beliefs and practices. If we are not 'cleaving unto' him, we will weakly submit to worldly pressures and perish. This will happen!

'The LORD will bring upon you all harmful things, until he has destroyed you' (v. 15). God, who fought for them in the land, will now turn and be their enemy if they embrace the practices which he brought them there to destroy. 'The anger of the LORD will burn against you, and you shall perish' (v. 16). We have here the warning of *divine punishment* of Israel.

May the Lord have mercy upon us and keep us 'cleaving unto' him with our whole hearts. This is why Joshua said, 'Love the LORD your God'. When we are in love with him, we are safe.

Joshua's last address to the nation (24:1–33)

'Then Joshua gathered all the tribes of Israel to Shechem and called for the elders of Israel, for their heads, for their judges, and for their officers; and they presented themselves before God' (v. 1). This time it was not just the leaders, but all Israel as well. It must have been a massive and moving gathering as the people came to hear their great leader speak to them for the last time.

Abraham had come to Shechem and it was there that God had said to him, 'To your descendants I will give this land' (Genesis 12:6–7). What a moment! Abraham built an altar at Shechem. Now, about 500 years later, the promise had come true and the land belonged to his descendants. Jacob purchased ground from the men of Shechem and also built an altar there (Genesis 33:18–20). It was to Mounts Gerizim and Ebal, very near to Shechem, that Israel had gathered to renew the covenant just after the victory at Ai. Joshua had built an altar on Mount Ebal (8:30–35). The gypsum on the rocks where the law had been written would still have been visible, and would have stirred vivid memories. To this geographically central spot, with its hallowed memories reaching down the centuries, the tribes gathered.

Tracing God's goodness (vv. 1–13)

Joshua begins his speech by speaking as if the words were those of God himself:

- 'I took your father Abraham' (v. 3);
- 'I ... gave him Isaac' (v. 3);
- 'To Isaac I gave Jacob and Esau' (v. 4);
- 'To Esau I gave the mountains of Seir' (v. 4);

- 'I sent Moses and Aaron' (v. 5);
- 'I plagued Egypt' (v. 5);
- 'I brought you out' (v. 5);
- 'Then I brought your fathers out of Egypt' (v. 6);
- 'He ... brought the sea upon them, and covered them' (v. 7);
- 'Your eyes saw what I did in Egypt' (v. 7);
- 'I brought you into the land of the Amorites' (v. 8);
- 'I gave them into your hand' (v. 8);
- 'I destroyed them from before you' (v. 8);
- 'I delivered you out of his [the king of Moab's] hand' (v. 10);
- 'I delivered them [the nations in Canaan] into your hand' (v. 11);
- 'I sent the hornet before you' (v. 12);
- 'I have given you a land for which you did not labour' (v. 13).

A further analysis of this passage reveals that:

- God *chose* Israel (vv. 1–4). God says, 'I took ... Abraham from the other side of the River' (i.e. the Euphrates).
- God *delivered* Israel (vv. 5–7). Joshua recounts the plagues in Egypt, the flight from Egypt and the successful crossing of the Red Sea.
- God *rescued* Israel (vv. 8–10). God rescued them from the hand of the soothsayer Balaam, as well as from the king of Moab.
- God *empowered* Israel (vv. 11–12) to conquer all the tribes which are listed here.
- God *enriched* Israel (v. 13). He gave them the land, the cities, the vineyards and olive groves.

These are the acts of God in the history of Israel. Israel had no basis for boasting, self-confidence or congratulating themselves. Everything that they had received was from God. Salvation is of God. We do not merit it; we do not deserve it; we could not work for it; we could not earn it; it is all of grace—the free unmerited favour of God. God saw us in our sins, and came to our aid in Christ. Oh, what a Saviour we have! Jesus! Our wonderful Lord!

Confronting God's standards (vv. 14–23)

JOSHUA'S STARK PROPOSITION—'CHOOSE' (VV. 14–15)

Joshua said,

> Now therefore, fear the LORD; serve him in sincerity and in truth, and put away the gods which your fathers served on the other side of the River and in Egypt. Serve the LORD! And if it seems evil to you to serve the LORD, choose for yourselves this day whom you will serve, whether the gods which your fathers served that were on the other side of the River, or the gods of the Amorites, in whose land you dwell.

The people were nominally serving *Yahweh*, but in reality they served other gods too. They were to serve God 'in sincerity' (no hypocrisy), 'and in truth' (honestly and with integrity). There was to be separation from all false gods. The choice was to be immediate—'this day'. 'Today' they must choose!

This confrontation must have been a mighty shock! Suddenly it was in their face! When people are confronted with God's terms they sometimes blame the preacher for being so personal when they should rather seek the Lord! The summons of Joshua speaks as loudly today as it did then.

The gods he mentions here are, firstly, those beyond the River, that is the Euphrates: the gods that Abraham served when he dwelt in Ur of the Chaldees, the Babylonian gods. Amazingly they had maintained this allegiance! Secondly, he speaks of the gods of Egypt. They are the gods of the Nile, the sun, the land and the sky. Thirdly, he speaks of the gods of the Amorites, in whose land they dwell. These were gods which demanded the sacrifice of their children, and which were served with cultic prostitution. They were dreadful and immoral gods.

The clear demand was to serve the Lord. If they served the Lord they would have to get rid of their other gods which they were worshipping. They were to choose to serve the Lord intelligently, decisively and willingly. If that was unacceptable, their choice was not between the Lord and the other gods, it was between the different sets of gods! They were called upon to choose to serve the gods of Babylon or the gods of the Amorites. 'That is your choice—choose,' said Joshua. Joshua was using shock treatment. This was exclusion! This was radical stuff! Was Joshua forbidding them from worshipping the Lord? 'No! No! Joshua, what are you saying to us?'

JOSHUA'S CLEAR DECLARATION (V. 15)

'But as for me and my house, we will serve the LORD.' This is one of the greatest statements to come from the mouth of this great man.

This was a *public* declaration of his faith. All could know that he served the Lord. No one would misunderstand where he stood. Joshua said, 'I have chosen! I am not serving other gods—No! I am serving the Lord.'

It was a *personal* declaration. He nailed his colours to the mast. Long ago Joshua had chosen to serve the Lord, and he would continue to do so. He was on the Lord's side, completely and forever! It was not only a once-and-for-all choice, it was also a series of choices made throughout life. His choices for God were personal and permanent.

It was a *proven* declaration. Joshua was no hypocrite. There was an integrity with their leader that none could dispute. Everyone knew of Joshua's transparency and truthfulness. The weight of an honest and pure life drove his words home.

It was a *paternal* declaration. How wonderful that Joshua could say, 'As for me and my house'! His family was united behind him. 'They have all chosen to follow the Lord.'

It was a *passionate* declaration. Joshua had brought the whole nation together. All who heard his clear declaration would never forget it. They would relate to their yet-to-be-born children how Joshua had stood before the whole nation and had testified that he was serving the Lord. This would reverberate down the generations.

It was a *purposeful* declaration. He had stood alone with Caleb many years ago, and had borne the wrath of a mutinous nation. Now, once again, he stands alone and declares before them all that whatever *they* are doing, he will not serve idols! His stand would surely bring many of them to the same dedicated position.

Elijah on Mount Carmel (1 Kings 18:21) called for a decision, and here Joshua also calls for a decision. He is demanding that they serve the Lord, but if they turn aside from him, they will have to choose to serve some deity, albeit a corrupt one. These two passages give credence to the preacher's challenge to people to come now to the Lord.

That decision will not save us, but it is a vital part of the whole plan of salvation. Jesus said, 'Come', and we must come. In the far country the prodigal son decided to arise and go to his father. He put his decision into action, returned home and was forgiven and restored. He decided, and then actually returned. People must therefore respond to God's invitation, decide, and then put that decision into action and actually come for salvation and radical blessing. That is a transaction of faith. Salvation is all of grace, so our coming is also of grace. Here again, divine sovereignty mingles with human responsibility.

ISRAEL'S INDIGNANT RESPONSE (VV. 16–18)

'So the people answered and said: "Far be it from us that we should forsake the LORD to serve other gods … We also will serve the LORD, for he is our God."' They were caught out and were startled at the thought of falling away from God. They were incensed. How dare Joshua ban them from the worship of their God? 'God took us from the house of bondage. You have no right to close the door of worship and service to us, Joshua. No! We will serve the Lord! You call us all the way to Shechem to tell us that we may not serve the Lord. Sorry, Joshua, but we *will* serve the Lord!'

JOSHUA'S ADAMANT REFUSAL (VV. 19–20)

'But Joshua said to the people, "You cannot serve the LORD, for he is a holy

God. He is a jealous God.'" 'You *cannot* serve God.' What a shocking refusal! Their glib and ready response was suspect. Joshua was saying that, if they were serving their idols, it was impossible for them to serve the Lord as well. To serve him is to discard all other gods. If he is served, no one or nothing else can be served. It is all or nothing! Israel must give themselves altogether to God, or not at all. God said, 'You shall have no other gods before me' (Exodus 20:3).

Joshua's objective was not to drive them away from God, but to shock them into the realization of their condition and thereby draw them back to him. If they did not return to God, he would do them harm (v. 20). Judgement awaits those who turn away from God.

So many today serve other gods and try to make a deal with God, attempting to accommodate their deviations. If you are joined to your idols—your home, your car or whatever—you cannot serve God. You need to be swept clean of all the offensive material to be able to serve the Lord.

ISRAEL'S CONTINUING INSISTENCE (V. 21)

'And the people said to Joshua, "No, but we will serve the LORD!"' Even after Joshua's strong words they continued to assert their right to serve the Lord. He had made the conditions perfectly clear, and now it was for them to respond to the burden which he had shared with them, which was the reason why he had brought them all to Shechem.

JOSHUA'S FINAL DEMAND AND THEIR RESPONSE (VV. 22–24)

'So Joshua said to the people, "You are witnesses against yourselves that you have chosen the LORD for yourselves, to serve him." And they said, "We are witnesses!" "Now therefore," he said, "put away the foreign gods which are among you, and incline your heart to the LORD God of Israel."' Joshua had said all he could. They must now take the initiative and close in with God. 'And the people said to Joshua, "The LORD our God we will serve, and his voice we will obey!"' They still had not promised to do away with their gods, but at least they had come to some sort of a commitment and were prepared to put this into practice.

Renewing God's covenant (vv. 25–28)

Three times the people affirmed their wish to serve the Lord (vv. 16–18,21,24). Joshua took them at their word and made a covenant with them. So that they would not forget this renewal of the covenant, he 'wrote these words in the Book of the Law of God' (v. 26). He then took a large stone and 'set it up ... under the oak that was by the sanctuary of the LORD.' The stone would 'be a witness to you, lest you deny your God.' Having completed this exercise, Joshua sent the people home, 'each to his own inheritance.'

'Israel served the LORD all the days of Joshua, and all the days of the elders who outlived Joshua' (v. 31), indicating the enormous impact that Joshua's life had had upon the nation. This is a great tribute to Joshua. What an influence he had! Do our lives leave an impression of godliness, an impact that will linger long after we are gone?

Joshua's fears about the spiritual condition of the nation were well-founded, for soon they 'served the Baals and Asherahs' (Judges 3:7). God sold them into the hand of the king of Mesopotamia. After eight years of bondage, they cried to the Lord for deliverance and he raised up a deliverer in the person of Othniel, Caleb's son-in-law. This would have been a short time after Joshua's death, for Othniel was still able to conquer and thereafter to judge Israel for forty years.

What a pity that they did not obey God in the first place and cleanse the land of the nations which were there! Those nations which remained led them into all the sins which they had come to destroy. Israel fell victim to the results of their own disobedience. When we disobey God, the results are far reaching. The price of disobedience is far greater than the price of obedience.

Burying God's servants (vv. 29–33)

There are three burials at the close of the book:

- Joshua died, being 110 years old, and was buried in his own inheritance.
- Eleazar the son of Aaron died, and they buried him in the property of Phinehas, his son, in Ephraim.
- The bones of Joseph were buried at Shechem in the plot of ground that Jacob had bought long ago.

The era of Joshua had come to an end, but the influence of that godly, obedient, faithful and choice man of God lives on and touches our lives even today! May these lessons stimulate us to a closer and more obedient walk with our God as we continue to follow him.

Amen and amen!

Bibliography

Agnew, Milton S., *The Better Covenant* (Kansas City: Beacon Hill Press, 1975).

Applebee, Denis, *When I Tread the Verge of Jordan* (Marion, IN: World Gospel Mission, 1988).

Blackaby, Henry and Richard, *Called to be God's Leader* (Nashville, TN: Thomas Nelson Inc., 2004).

Boice, James Montgomery, *Joshua: We will Serve the Lord* (Old Tappan, NJ: Fleming H. Revel, 1989).

Butler, John G., *Joshua* (Clinton, OH: LBC Publications, 1996).

Butler, Trent C., *Joshua* (Word Biblical Commentary) (Waco, TX: Word Books, 1983).

Clarke, Adam, *Clarke's Commentary: The Old Testament*, Vol. 2 (New York: Abingdon Press, 1820).

Davis, Dale Ralph, *Joshua: No Falling Words* (Tain: Christian Focus Publications, 2003).

Ellison, H. L., *Joshua–2 Samuel* (London: Scripture Union, 1966).

Epp, Theodore H., *Joshua: Victorious by Faith* (Lincoln, NB: Back to the Bible, 1983).

Gray, John, *Joshua, Judges, Ruth* (Grand Rapids: Eerdmans, 1986).

Hastings, James, *The Great Texts of the Bible: Deuteronomy–Esther* (London: T & T Clark, 1911).

Henry, Matthew, *Commentary: Deuteronomy to Esther*, Vol. 2 (London: Marshall Bros, 1710).

Hess, Richard, *Joshua* (Leicester: IVP, 1996).

Huffman, John, *Joshua* (Mastering the OT) (Dallas: Word Publishers, 1986).

Keil, C. F. and Delitzsch, F., *Commentary on the Old Testament*, Vol. 2 (Grand Rapids: Eerdmans, 1978).

Lawrence, Brother, *The Practice of the Presence of God* (London: Samuel Baxter & Sons, n.d.).

MacDonald, William, *Believer's Bible Commentary* (Nashville: Thomas Nelson, 1992).

MacLaren, Alexander, *Expositions on Deuteronomy, Joshua, Judges, Ruth, and 1 Samuel* (London: Hodder & Stoughton, 1906).

McAlpine, Campbell, *The Practice of Biblical Meditation* (n.d.).

Meyer, F. B., *Joshua and the Land of Promise* (London: Marshall & Scott, n.d.).

Meyer, F. B., *The Way into the Holiest* (London: Marshall, Morgan & Scott, 1950).

Mulder, Chester O., *Joshua*, Beacon Bible Commentary (Kansas City: Beacon Hill Press, 1965).

Murray, Andrew, *The State of the Church* (London: James Nisbet & Co., n.d.).

Murray, Andrew, *The Holiest of All* (London: Marshall, Morgan & Scott, 1976).

Nelson, Richard D., *Joshua* (Louisville, KY: Westminster John Knox Press, 1997).

Newell, William R., *Hebrews Verse by Verse* (Chicago: Moody Press, 1947).

Ogilvie, Lloyd J., *Joshua* (The Communicator's Commentary) (Waco, TX: Word, 1986).

Palmer, Phoebe, *Full Salvation* (Salem, OH: Schmul Publishers, n.d.).

Parker, Joseph, *Joshua–Judges*, The People's Bible (London: Hodder & Stoughton, 1896).

Peckham, C. N., *When God Guides* (Edinburgh: The Faith Mission, 1983).

Peckham, C. N., *From Defeat to Victory* (Edinburgh: The Faith Mission, 1993).

Peckham, C. N., *The Authority of the Bible* (Tain: Christian Focus Publications, 1999).

Peckham, C. N., *Scattered Pearls* (Edinburgh: C. N. Peckham, 2004).

Phillips, John, *Exploring Hebrews* (Chicago: Moody Press, 1977).

Pink, Arthur W., *Joshua* (Chicago: Moody Press, 1973).

Rea, John, *The Wycliffe Bible Commentary* (London: Oliphants, 1969).

Redpath, Alan, *Victorious Christian Living* (London: Pickering & Inglis, 1956).

Rodgers, Thomas R., *The Panorama of the Old Testament* (Newburgh, IN: Impact Press, 1988).

Sanders, J. Oswald, *The Christian's Promised Land* (Eastbourne: Kingsway, 1984).

Scroggie, W. Graham, *The Land and Life of Rest* (London: Pickering & Inglis, 1950).

Simpson, A. B., *The Land of Promise* (Alexandria, LA: Lamplighter Publications, n.d.).

Simpson, A. B., *Joshua* (Christ in the Bible Series) (Harrisburg, PA: Christian Publications, n.d.).

Smith, James, *Handfuls on Purpose*, Vol. 4 (London: Pickering & Inglis, n.d.).

Spurgeon, C. H., *The Treasury of the Old Testament*, Vol. 1 (London: Marshall, Morgan & Scott, n.d.).

(No author given) *The Pulpit Commentary*, Vol. 2 (Numbers 21–1 Samuel) (AP & A, n.d.).

Tucker, Gene M., *The Book of Joshua* (Cambridge University Press, 1974).

Way, Arthur S., *Letters of St Paul and Hebrews* (London: MacMillan & Co. Ltd, 1921).

Wiersbe, Warren W., *Be Strong: Joshua* (Amersham-on-the-Hill: Scripture Press, 1993).

Williams, Isaac, *The Characters of the Old Testament* (London: Longmans, Green & Co., 1899).

Witherby, H. Forbes, *The Book of Joshua* (London: James Nisbet & Co., n.d.).

Woudstra, Marten H., *The Book of Joshua* (Grand Rapids: William Eerdmans, 1981).